The
MYSTERY
— OF —
KNOWLEDGE

Modern Cognitive Theory on
Integrated Cognitive Structure

DR. MOHAMED HASSAN AL SHARQAWI

authorHOUSE®

AuthorHouse™
1663 Liberty Drive
Bloomington, IN 47403
www.authorhouse.com
Phone: 1 (800) 839-8640

Published by AuthorHouse 01/10/2018

ISBN: 978-1-5462-1973-6 (sc)
ISBN: 978-1-5462-1974-3 (hc)
ISBN: 978-1-5462-1972-9 (e)

Library of Congress Control Number: 2017918824

Print information available on the last page.

Contents

**To my mom,
wife, and family**

(Knowledge is wealth, power, health, and excellence in life.)

Dr. Mohamed Hassan Al Sharqawi

ADVICE

If you ever feel lethargic, do not
continue reading this book.
Leave it, and then come back to it when
you find that you have a predisposition
and a desire for doing so.
With each chapter, you will find what will
raise your curiosity and refresh your mind.

AUTHOR

PREFACE

To those who move ambitiously and assiduously to knowledge, inviting others to do so, and spend their lives building knowledge, I extend greetings from the depth of my heart. To the knowledge lovers, who exerted their best efforts and confronted difficulties to achieve knowledge, even when it took forever...Greetings to all the innovators around the world from the Great Rift Valley.[1]

Through knowledge we may know how our ancestors lived millions of years ago. Let us learn more and more, and in doing so, restructure knowledge. Without knowledge life would be meaningless. Knowledge is the key to light, innovation, and a better future.

The initial thoughts to this literature emerged five years ago. It was intended to be a reference in which we all find a way to our goals and needs. Knowledge is broader, more comprehensive, and more expansive. Our need for knowledge is profound, significant, and has a far-reaching impact. It does not found its structure and pillars unless we participate in getting those pillars established according to the specialty, interest, abilities, determination, and imagination of each of us. It is not based on an individual or a specialty, a certain color or ethnicity. An individual, who seeks to advance his abilities and talents, will find the answer to his ambition in knowledge. It leads us to know how to be, how to organize, how to manage, how to produce, how to make, how to grow, and how to invest in our knowledge. Further, it shows us how to maximize our

---

[1] The Great Rift Valley is located in North East Ethiopia, in Africa. Geologists believe that this is the place where the first human was found. In this valley, deep cracking occurred along six thousand kilometers and it almost split Africa into two halves, and so it is called the Great Rift Valley, or the Great African Rift.

capital market value and how to achieve excellence and advantage over others. Can anyone achieve success, superiority and excellence without cognitive structure, management, investment and engineering? Let us be part of knowledge, be the knowledge makers, or in more exact terms – the makers of civilization.

CHAPTER I

In this chapter:

- The meaning of knowledge
- The story of "Michael"
- The secret of knowledge
- What is the significance of Michael's story and its relationship with knowledge?
- How does knowledge move inside the mind?
- How do we define knowledge?
- Desire and its relationship with knowledge
- Significance of desire in cognitive structure
- Cases for measuring desire
- Knowledge deposits
- Conclusion

The meaning of knowledge

Writers, authors, scientists, and researchers have dealt with knowledge unhindered, seeking it in various theories, philosophies, and academic research that are so distant from the reality of practical life. I hope that my research on knowledge reaches every soul that desires knowledge eagerly and excitedly - regardless of its location, specialization, and goal.

Knowledge is the maker of creativity, entrepreneurship, excellence, value, and life.

Each part of this literature, from beginning to end, will be the blocks that we will use simply, block by block, to explain the modern theory of knowledge.

Modern Cognitive Theory on Integrated Cognitive Structure

Stem Cells Cognitive Theory (SCC)

The story of Michael

Michael is a firefighter who grew up in a quiet, stable family, that was always hungry for excellence. His father was a major general in the army, who was well-known for his dedication to his work, sincerity, loyalty, as well as his creativity, which distinguished him from others. His mother was a doctor in the city. She strongly believed in commitment and scientific research, and even encouraged it. She was known for being an active reader, inspired greatly by the Brontë sisters, who believed that reading is the food of the mind and the point where its spirit and creativity starts. She thought it was the door for acquiring concentration and mind agility.

One day the city declared a state of emergency due to the high temperatures, that could potentially cause a lot of fires. The warning alarm rang when Michael was on duty and everyone rushed toward their machines and equipment. The firetrucks headed to the scene and within seven minutes Michael and the team were at the scene. It was an old sports club that was on fire. Michael inspected the place, and ordered his team to enter the building and control the fire. Within five minutes the team were in the final stages of controlling the blaze when suddenly, and before they could finish, Michael made an odd and unexpected decision – everyone was to come out immediately. A few seconds later the whole building had collapsed!

Michael's team had survived, miraculously escaping from certain death, but how did it happen? It was just a few seconds between their exit and the collapse of the entire building.

How did Michael know what will happen?

How did Michael know what will happen? Is that knowledge? Is that what knowledge makes? If that is the product of knowledge, how can we learn this from Michael? How can we take advantage of this incident on a personal level? What is the role of society and environment in the construction, formation and accumulation of knowledge? Are knowledge-makers the builders of civilization? All these questions and others wander through our minds as we read Michael's incident.

Michael's team were not working alone in the management of this incident. There were other teams on standby, following the details of what was happening and waiting to see if they can be of assistance. In addition, there was a chopper that was filming this incident. After Michael and his team completed their mission successfully, they were summoned for an investigation…

What is the signification of Michael's story and its relationship with knowledge?

How many operations, events and stories may be more wonderful than this or more educational but due to our rapid life styles we pass it without learning from its successes and failures. How and why did it happen? What is its significance? What are the learned lessons? What are the pros and cons? How can we avoid repeating the mistakes and how can we take advantage of its sources of strength?

It is the time for us to rid ourselves of the practice or the belief that audits, investigations or inquiries are a means of accusing an individual or honoring someone and insulting another. When we do that we are ready to capture the essence of knowledge so that knowledge-makers can mature and we can have the foundations of a healthy and educated society.

Back to Michael's investigation. They collected all the pictures of the incident and began summoning eyewitnesses. Firefighters were called and asked to describe in detail what happened? When Michael was called in, he was asked:

- How much time did it take between getting notified about the fire and leaving with the fire engines?
- How much time did it take to get to the scene?
- How did he assess the fire?
- What was his plan for handling and controlling the fire?
- How were the standards he adhered to compared with international standards?
- Why did he make a sudden decision for his team to get out, even though they were about to finish extinguishing the fire?

Michael answered calmly, wisely, and very politely. He explained how he felt that this fire was different from any other fire he had seen or dealt with in the past twenty years. While his team was inside, he had a sudden feeling of anxiety that he couldn't pin the reason for, but then he saw three strange phenomena that bothered him too much:

(1.) The first phenomenon: The fire was changing to an orange color, unlike any other fire he had previously experienced.
(2.) The second phenomenon: The air rushed into the building when the doors opened, instead of rushing out as usual.
(3.) The third phenomenon: This fire did not release any sound. Usually, fires crackle while they burn oxygen.

He analyzed these 3 phenomena as they happened rapidly in front of him and felt uneasy and anxious, and therefore took the decision to bring the team out immediately. The investigation team could not move past this point that provoked puzzlement and astonishment. How did Michael's mind reach such a decision?

How does knowledge move inside the mind?

On the next day, psychologists were called in to answer this question: what happened exactly to push him to make such a decision? The scientists came up with the following answer:

When the forebrain is faced with a problem or a crisis, the conscious brain can't decide fast enough, so the forebrain resorts to scanning and reviewing quickly all the previous images seen by it, which are similar to this situation or incident, and compares them with what the person is facing at the moment. The forebrain can do this in less than a part of a second. In Michael's case, his brain resorted to comparing between the fire in the sports club and all the other fires that he had witnessed over his career. In a blink of an eye, Michael's brain had noticed these phenomena, which resulted in his feeling of uneasiness or what people might describe as a hunch. Thereby, Michael's decision was a reaction to this hunch which was a result of him trying to analyze his surroundings.

Knowledge is the product of the brains' active movement since the early phases of an individual's life. This movement activates neurons, centers of thinking, imagination, association, deduction, understanding, and alertness to details. It further activates the neurological electrochemical charge and the neural links; thus, creating talents and abilities, making it a cognitive container.

If Michael hadn't grown, habituated, and trained since his early years to use his mind to inspect what surrounds him and to ask about ambiguous things, his mind would not have been opened to new talents and gifts. After all, how could concentration and intuition suddenly emerge in a grown-up after his personality had formed? Furthermore, knowledge can't originate from emptiness and inactivity, without using mind or imagination.

Unless Michael had previous experiences in which he interacted with all his consciousness, talents, and thoughts, his perception would not have reached a point where he would be getting hunches upon which he can act. His family were a big part in developing the layers of his cognitive container since his early life. The society and the surrounding environment further contributed in this structure. Thus, when these signs appeared to him during the fire, his anxiety and subsequent decision which rescued his team, were the normal outcome of long-time structuring of his mental container.

After investigating the fire, it turned out that the fire had burnt up all the oxygen in the enclosed space, which thus led to the explosion.

The most important point is that what happened to Michael is not just limited to him. His story is the story of humans and knowledge since man walked this planet. Our ancestor's experiences were transmitted to us and that is how humanity has gotten to where it is today.

So how does knowledge form?

How do we define knowledge?

If I asked you to examine the story of Michael carefully to deduce a simple, full, and accurate definition of knowledge, what would you say? Below are a few lines where you could write out your thoughts.

Knowledge is:

....

....

When I asked this question in a lecture I was giving, I got various interesting answers. Two of those were:

* Knowledge is the desire to use your mind for learning and understanding, then practicing what you learn, followed by gaining experience, then updating and developing this knowledge every day. The last stage is using this knowledge for innovation.
* Knowledge is a compelling and nonstop desire of understanding, research, and cognition. In addition to that, it is the patience for acquiring further knowledge, understanding, action and practice, with continuous concentration, realization, imagination, visualization, and thinking. The next step is development to reach the most important part of knowledge, which is innovation.

It is crucial to understand though, that knowledge cannot be explained as an addition of separate components. So, you cannot explain it as:

............+......... = Knowledge

Desire and its relationship to knowledge

I was once asked: how can the desire for knowledge be continuously burning and vigilant? A continuous and burning willingness does not stop. It may calm down, but it always lights back up. For example, if you want to be an athlete who achieves a world record in bodybuilding what would you do? You may train strongly and enthusiastically for one or two days or even a week, but it could be that you stopped training because you were busy, lazy or just lacked the will to continue. So, will you gain any benefit from having trained for a day, two days or for a week? Will your muscles gain benefit? Will your chest become muscular, if you got distracted, busy or stopped your training?

How far you go will depend most importantly on the strength of your will. This strength, that grows as you imagine yourself breaking this record, will renew the energy of your brain (your cognitive container), thus renewing your nerve cells accordingly, making its links become more active. It is a power that overcomes any difficulties, challenges or pain. The endurance of a person who has willingness and motivation differs like night and day from someone who doesn't. Think about people who have succeeded and achieved distinctive achievements and innovations. Einstein never stopped thinking, imagining, inquiring or searching for even a moment. He would ask and re-ask the question, until he found an answer that satisfied him. He died on his bed at seventy-six years old while he held his pen and notebook still searching for answers. This is knowledge and this is how it dominates your life.

Why is it not enough to mention endurance and strength of will? This is because they do not sufficiently express what we want to reach. Patience and endurance may be a result of routine. Some people are highly disciplined, have the power of endurance, but they are not often creative or innovative. Such an individual might not know how to act in a situation that requires wisdom, intuition, and maybe innovation. But, if in addition to will and endurance, there is a need for constant development and the accumulation of new knowledge, along with a willingness to learn and to search for new things, this attribute, as a result, takes a turn for the better.

<u>Significance of desire in cognitive structure</u>

To understand the significance of desire in the cognitive structure, look at the following image:

Figure 1: Two students in a classroom

The picture shows two students in a classroom after being asked a question. Student 2 raises her hand while student 1 is sitting next to her. Which student do you feel has the bigger desire to learn? Look at the extended hand movement of student no. 2 and analyze its significance. If desire and eagerness are reflected on people, this is probably what it would look like. Now analyze the eyes of student 1. It seems like he is thinking of something outside the realm of that room, probably even the school. There is a lack of interest in his eyes that tell me that he would probably not hear anything the teacher explains, let alone retain it. On the other hand, look at the compassion and excitement of the second pupil, as if she wants to scream out the answer at the top of her voice.

Cases for measuring desire

The first case:

Figure 2: Two men at different emotional states

In the above images try to measure the desire reflected by the body language of the two men above.

....

....

....

....

The second case:

Figure 3: A slam-dunk

In the above image try to measure the desire and passion reflected by the body language of the basketball player above.

....

....

Figure 4: A depressed person

Now imagine if we gave the person in this **figure 4** sportswear, and we asked him to take advantage of the opportunity available to him by scoring a goal similar to the goal made by the basketball player in the second case **(figure 3)**. Do you think he would utilize the chance given to him or would he lose this opportunity? Would he have the desire and passion for it?

A similar scenario happened a little over one hundred years ago, in 1914, in one of the streets of London. William was a scientist in Epidemiology and his colleague, Harry, was a specialist in gynecology and obstetrics. While walking together down a street a lady passes next to them while they were in the middle of a conversation about skin color and traders who benefit from slave trade. Harry interrupts William saying that this woman is 4 months pregnant. William was surprised and asked his friend if she was one of his patients to which Harry answered no. To sate his curiosity William ran up to the woman, and after introducing Harry and himself, he asked her if she was in fact 4 months pregnant. The woman was taken aback at this but then said with a smile that it was true. Her doctor had just given her the good news. William turned to Harry with a shocked face, but Harry smiled and explained that it was his love and passion for his work that made him so eager to know everything about it and that made him so good to the point that he could tell how far along a woman is by just looking at her.

This passion and eagerness is one of the secrets of knowledge.

Knowledge deposits in the mind

The human brain is thought to have 100 billion neurons and ten times more glial cells, but still the absolute number of neurons and glial cells in the human brain is unknown. [2] It is the center of the nervous

---

[2] Equal numbers of neuronal and no neuronal cells make the human brain an isometric ally scaled-up primate brain J Comp Neurol.2009 Apr 10; 513(5):532-41. Doi: 10.1002/cne.21974. http://www.ncbi.nlm.nih.gov/pubmed/19226510

system in humans, and controls memory, vision, learning, thoughts, and awareness among other activities. It is the most complicated part in the human body, and may be the most complicated thing in the universe. It is also the place where knowledge is built, where the nerve cells grow and regenerate, and become active with our talents, increasing our intuition, and accelerating the strength and dimensions of our understanding. Michaels' cognitive container would not have formed in the way we saw in his story if it had not been for presence of his family, the surrounding environment, and the community, which would have made his story end in a completely different way. We will not be able to deal properly with this cognitive container, or understand its composition and construction, if we ignore the effects of family, community, and the environment on the formation and building of this cognitive container.

The cognitive container of Michael did not form instantaneously. The brain just like everything in nature must follow the rules of the universe. There were layers and sediments forming, following different interactions and conversations. It is a process that cannot be hurried or rushed. When people look at the pyramids in Egypt, a lot of them start wondering about how they were built and raised but I always wonder – how did those rocks form?

Thinking about that made me then start to wonder – how is our knowledge formed? What is the link between the formation of knowledge and the composition of the limestone rocks that made the pyramids in Egypt, one of the wonders of the world? You will probably be as surprised as I was when I realized that the answer to both questions is the same. In fact, it is one of the constants in our universe.

The answer to the 1st question is 50,000 years. That was how long it took for those limestones to form. Let us try to see how that happened.

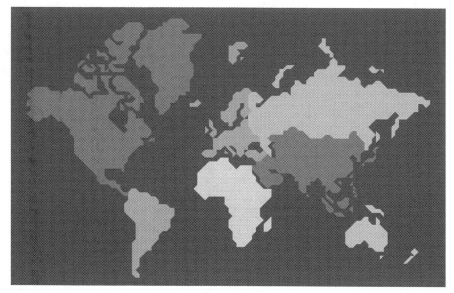

Figure 5: Pangea

Pangea

Millions of years ago, the continents were all in the form of one block of land that was called Pangea. Pangea meant mother. Then this mother began gradual secession that resulted in its current form, as shown above in **figure 5**.[3]Africa separated from South America and the Atlantic Ocean extended, forming the gap between the old and the new world. On the other hand, in the north of Africa, what is now contemporary Egypt was still under the old sea, located at the bottom of sea creatures called Nomayt.[4]These creatures consisted of shells of calcium and carbon. They accumulated at the bottom of the sea for millions of years, forming limestone as a result. It was this limestone that was used by the ancient Egyptians in the construction of the Great Pyramids.

---

[3] History of the World - in Two Hours (Documentary) - Written and Directed by Douglas J. Cohen Editor - Kevin Browne
[4] History of the World - in Two Hours (Documentary) - Written and Directed by Douglas J. Cohen Editor - Kevin Browne

In the same way that these limestones took years and years to form and calcify, so does anything in this universe of any value or importance. It takes years to perfect. Knowledge follows the same rules. It takes years for all the layers to from and strengthen; it's a process that starts at birth.

Conclusion

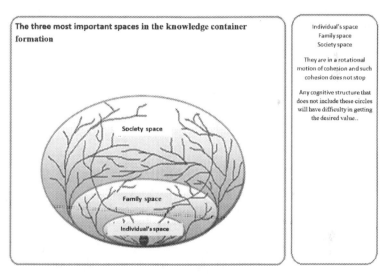

The three most important spaces in the knowledge container formation

Individual's space
Family space
Society space

They are in a rotational motion of cohesion and such cohesion does not stop

Any cognitive structure that does not include these circles will have difficulty in getting the desired value..

Society space

Family space

Individual's space

Figure 6: The three spaces that form
the knowledge container

Michael's mind (his cognitive container), started developing, before he was even born, from the genetic coding of his parents. When he came out to the world, it developed further through his interaction with his environment. The layers will start forming and strengthening with every incident he goes through, every person he talks to and everything he sees around him. The individual, the family, and then the environment: these are the 3 most important players in the formation of a person's perceptions, biases, and knowledge. They collectively constitute the broad and fundamental lines of an individual's personality, his impressions, perceptions, and how he receives and communicates with life.

CHAPTER II

In this chapter we will discuss:

- Knowledge space.
- How to deal with knowledge space through integral knowledge building.
- The distinction between knowledge spaces and the hollowness of some spaces between individuals.
- The knowledge spaces that form the knowledge container of the individual.

Knowledge space

Knowledge space "Knowledge Ba"

The Japanese Philosopher, Kitaro Nishida[5], was the first to talk about the subject of knowledge space, after which it was introduced by Nonaka and Konno. The word "Ba" is of Japanese origin. It means place in English. When knowledge was first introduced as a modern science in the mid-nineties, its concept was derived from business companies and principles of businessmen in major international companies. This space was dealt with as a space of relations and frictions between individuals in the work environment and work-teams (shared space). This shared space can either be physical such as offices and workshops, or virtual via internal and external electronic networks and other forms.

This is what is meant by knowledge space. It is the place where ideas meet and interact to discuss an issue. Accordingly, the space here represents an incubator for knowledge inside organizations and companies. Another issue they return to, is whether the knowledge is tacit or explicit knowledge. When knowledge is apparent and explicit, it is independent from its knowledge space. Yet when knowledge is tacit and hidden, it becomes connected and cohesive with its knowledge space.

How to deal with knowledge space through integral knowledge building?

How do we look at, and deal with, knowledge space according to stem cells cognitive (SCC) theory?

---

[5] Nishida Kitarō - *First published Fri Feb 25, 2005; substantive revision Fri May 18, 2012* http://plato.stanford.edu/entries/nishida-kitaro/

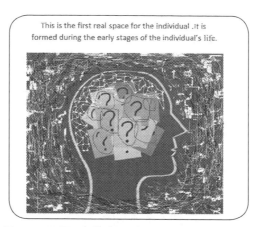

This is the first real space for the individual .It is formed during the early stages of the individual's life.

Figure 7: Knowledge space in an individual

Scholars who talked about the individual's knowledge space, discussed the matter in terms of the actuality of business inside companies, whether indoors, i.e. offices, and workshops, or via electronic networks of all kinds. Looking at the knowledge space through this scene is regarded as a violation of the entire knowledge space scene. It violates how it has been created, formed, and how it communicates. The actuality of companies with its multiple spaces only represent a small shot within the range of the individual's long knowledge space. We will often discuss the individual's knowledge space throughout this book in all its sections. It will have a huge role when we discuss the integral knowledge space.

In an individual, the knowledge space's formation, creation, and structure goes through several long extensive phases, since the early genetic stages of a fetus. Next, throughout childhood and what an individual gets exposed to within the family, the surrounding environment, and society with all its attendant circumstances causes more changes in the knowledge space. Then comes adolescence. Afterwards, the individual moves to a business space whether it is an organization, company or an entity. The lines of the individual's knowledge space are not discontinued in order to have separate intermittent spaces like a picture cut into pieces. It is a well-connected communicating world. The whole affects the parts. Still, the sum of its part is what shapes and produces the full space where the knowledge components and outcomes move.

The impact of the development of one's knowledge space shows in being quick-witted for example, or by having a feature that dominates and shows the individual's primary characteristics, or an extraordinary trait that distinguishes this person from others in a game, hobby, or any path in life. This growth is the integral knowledge building process.

The knowledge spaces and its distinct levels between individuals

What if some people do not carry much in their knowledge space, and you have to deal with them in some capacity? Let's imagine that we have a team member who does not have a solid base for creating his own knowledge space. As a result, we will probably be facing one or more of the challenges detailed below.

First challenge: to find a sharp distinction between the knowledge containers of each member of the team.

Second challenge: One of the members might not have a proper basis for the knowledge space of the group.

Third challenge: Half of the group has a firm strong knowledge space, while the rest lack this feature.

Fourth challenge: The majority of the team members do not have a basis for a highly valuable knowledge space.

If we supposedly assume that we are facing a machine (brain), then we are facing a device of complex formation and structure, where a huge amount of knowledge, energy, and millions of pictures, sounds, scents, memories, behaviors, words, situations, data, information, imagination, and stories are stored. The brain has it all, and more than that. The brain is a container, and a structure where interaction with life movement occurs.

We do not believe that, under any circumstance, we will have a device with which we can do whatever we like, and fill it with what we want.

Piaget, the brilliant Swiss scientist, has founded and established as part of his knowledge theory, that knowledge building is only created properly through two primary perspectives:

1   Mental structure
2   Mental function.

Michael, the hero in our first story, joined the organization with his mental structure already formed alongside all, or almost all, of his profound beliefs. The organization will probably enrich him, since the human brain is designed for learning, development, and reviving its cells on regular basis. He will be taught by means of regulations, instructions, practices, experiences, and training, the result of which will increase his knowledge. However, Michael will not be reshaped and restructured by the structure of the organization. It will not destroy what he bears in his mind. It will only make of him what he already is. It will not give him a new brain. Certainly, the organization takes part in the process of building and formation, yet this formation process will mainly depend on what he has in his mind; being ready, desirous, motivated, determined, with conceptions, potentials, and beliefs. No organization will be able to take off, or make radical changes to all of these elements, no matter what trends or preparations it has.

The director of "Eternal Sunshine of the Spotless mind", a sci-fi feature film, which won an Oscar had an interesting take on this. In the film, the writer and the director of the film fancied that modern technology serves an imaginary visionary role in reshaping the brain with respect to the erasure of some memories from the brain. It envisaged that this would happen between a loving couple, who meet, and due to clashes between them break up later on. Then both of them would want to erase the other party from his/her memory. So, each of them, without the knowledge of the other, visited a specialist physician. The physician succeeded in erasing the part of their memory that reminds him/ her of their ex-. But, surprisingly, they fall in love once again. As much as we would like this to be conceivable, this isn't something that is possible with our current technology.

<u>The knowledge spaces that form the knowledge container of the individual</u>

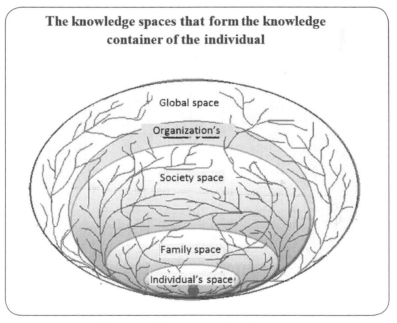

Figure 8: The spaces that form the individual knowledge container

When you examine the above drawing, imagine a column stretching from the red point that shows us the beginning of the formation of knowledge, going through the individual's space, with all its overlapping and overlaying layers and components. This might look complicated but for the brain, it is so accurate and precise. Besides, it is very fast in archiving, organization, maintenance, and revision. This red column passes by the family space, followed by the space of the society, its entities, its surrounding environment, and its influence. Finally, it passes through the organization's space until it reaches the global space.

CHAPTER III

In this chapter we will discuss:

- The fundamental factors affecting the cognitive structure process.
- The individual and his role in the cognitive structure process.
- Real-world example of the individual's role in the cognitive structure process.
- Family and their role in the cognitive structure process.
- A real-world example of the role of family in the cognitive structure process.
- The surrounding community and environment and their role in the cognitive structure process.
- Genes (heredity) and its role in the cognitive structure process.

The fundamental factors affecting building and forming the cognitive container

After discussing cognitive space, the next question would be: What are the main factors that affect the formation of the cognitive container?

There are key factors that play an active and important role in the construction and composition of the cognitive container (mind) starting from the embryonic stage and what follows, in terms of construction and development, until the character is formed and the outlines of the composition and mind are drawn.

These factors have been identified and arranged, through studying thousands of creative individuals throughout various historical epochs and civilizations. This study was inclusive of all types of human minds that have contributed to the construction of the different civilizations of the world, be they scientists, military leaders, politicians, businessmen, creative artists, writers, authors, researchers or explorers.

There are four fundamental components that play the role of the backbone in the construction of the cognitive container for the individual's mind:

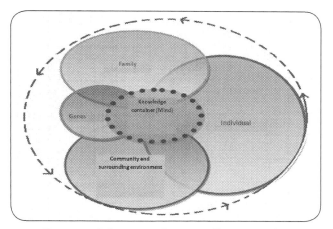

Figure 9: The main factors influencing the
construction and formation of cognitive awareness

The outer circle in **figure 9** represents the individual's role in the completion, maturation, care, continuation, enriching, and filling of his cognitive composition continuously.

The ordering of these components are as follows:

- The individual.
- The family
- The surrounding environment and community. This component includes the place where we live and surround us, the people that live in it, the terrain and characteristics that differentiates it, and the impact of this environment on all who live in it and its atmosphere. This further incorporates society, including all of its segments, the people living in it, with all the cultural, civilizational, ideological, and legal characteristics that distinguishes them.
- The genes (heredity).

First: the individual and his role in the cognitive structure process.

The individual here means the extent of his movement and his activity, his manner of behaving, determination, will, perseverance, ambition, and determination. Although this factor appears in the advanced stages experienced by the individual through his growth and development, it is still an active, vital and indispensable factor in all the studied cases. It is, however, the most dangerous factor and has the most powerful influence in the life of the cognitive container, which is why in terms of effect it has the largest size in the figure above.

Among all the other factors, the role of the individual in the continuation of his cognitive composition continuously is a complementary and essential role. Therefore, I make it interact with all the other components, represented by the outer circle that encircles all the other circles that are adherent to the individual, to represent the real role of the individual in the completion of his role in the construction of his cognitive container.

This outer circle is expressive about the never-ending role of the individual in the addition, care, follow-up, upgrading, and continuous furbishing of his cognitive construction. Without this circle, the other components will not achieve the desired results no matter how strong they are or how integral their role.

A real-world example about the role of the individual in cognitive construction

Let us look at an example of the role of the individual in cognitive construction.

Tom always hated reading as a boy. His mother was constantly trying to make him read and he hated that even more. He was preoccupied with television, video games, and football. His mother feared for him, seeing her son wasting his future and not investing in his mental development. So, she decided to play a trick on him. She started putting football magazines next to his bed and then started watching to see if he would read them. Over the whole week, he did not glance at the magazines, or even move them from their place like he was afraid to touch them. She wouldn't say anything but kept changing the magazines, so as to always have the most recent and attractive magazines with stories of players he idolizes inside them. After a while, she noticed he began skimming through them and after 2 months it developed to the point that he wouldn't sleep before browsing them. One day, she went a step further: she removed all the old magazines and didn't put new magazines in their place. Tom had to unhappily call his mother and ask where all the magazines were? Artfully, she concealed her smile like all mothers when they are being sly, and apologized to him saying that someone must have removed them. Rushing to her room she brought him a new stack and left without a word.

A week later, she wanted to place next to the magazines, an interesting and enjoyable novel so she decided on Wuthering Heights by Emily Bronte. But even she was surprised when he began read the story with a smile. He did not put the story down, or go out to play football all day. He continued reading until the next morning, and after he had finished he went to his mother and told her all about it.

Tom had been changed.

Reading changed Tom's thoughts and personality. He was like a person reborn, more active and vigorous with a strong desire to invest in his own self and time. Years later, this little boy who discovered his love for books became one of the most famous novelists of science fictions for teenagers: Tom Palmer.

Knowledge had taught him how to add value to himself, and he wanted to do the same for others, because Tom realized that the secret of building his own self as well as his mental faculties and strengthening his fount of knowledge lies in the value he adds to others and the principles he implants in them. Knowledge has taught him how to improve himself and hence to improve others. And just like Tom did, so can we all!

If we are discussing self-building as well as the challenges faced during this process it is important to know a little about Steve.

Steve embodied the individual role at building and forming his own self, even at challenging himself and discovering his own talents and abilities at the leadership level as well as other levels such as technology and worldwide technological excellence. He represented the personal success at unlocking, leading, directing, and promoting creative powers, even transferring these powers to people around him. He managed to build a company out of nothing and make it into a worldwide phenomenon. He was Steve Jobs (Apple Inc.)

Family and its role in the cognitive structure process

It is important to consider the family's role in building the cognitive awareness of a person, regarding orientation, education, care, and stimulation as well as observing talents. All these factors play an essential role in forming the cognitive container as well as the knowledge carrier inside the child. This is the stage in which their conceptions, personality, tendency, and activity are constructed. The effect of this factor (the family) starts from the fetal stage and the subsequent stages that begin with the early childhood phase that witnesses the child growth and the formation of his mental and body structure. It further continues into the last stage called "late childhood" in which the outlines of his personality manifest, followed by the adolescence phase.

The family has an important role in this respect, especially regarding the construction of a child's abilities and working on improving and promoting them. Unless the family considers the significance of its role, the results would be so difficult to imagine or treat. It is almost impossible to repair some of the disorders caused by family, except in cases where the surrounding environment attempts to play that role and repair some of the damage the family was responsible for.

Practical example of family's role within the cognitive structure process

The Bronte Sisters are a great example to portray the family's vital role within the cognitive structure process. It depicts the story of a miserable family, and how their cleverness and intellect emerged from the depths of their gloomy tragedy.

During the early part of the 19th century, there was a village called Haworth, located in the western part of Yorkshire, in the north of

England. It was a remote, poor, moist, and swampy village, where a lot of its inhabitants died before the age of six.

Fate drove Mr. Patrick to work as a priest in the village's church, which was surrounded by terrifying graves, desolate jungle, and moist and cold swamps. Patrick was a distinctive person, who was born in a very poor family in Northern Ireland. His father was a farmer, but with Patrick's cleverness, intelligence, and abilities he qualified to study in Cambridge University and then to work as a cleric. His wife Maria gave birth to six children during the period of 1814 to 1820, after which she died of tuberculosis. On her death bed, he made her an oath to never leave her children.

Patrick concealed his sufferings, wishes, and ambitions, and started teaching his children how to read and write. He spent time with them to draw letters, to decorate words and to read stories. Then in the evening, he would tell them stories and composes tales, so they were flying with their imagination to a better life full of wonders.

Days passed, and theirs were filled with story followed by story, lesson followed by lesson, and book followed by book. They spent their time in drawing, poetry, and music. Patrick was only attending liturgy in the church, and between them he would go home to spend time with his kids. When he became exhausted and needed someone to help him bear his burdens, their aunt started helping out. It was hard for the children to bear this with their aunt being a little bit harsh. So, they made a better world for themselves in their imagination, and they created their dreams and characters.

Charlotte, the elder sister, motivated them one day to try their hand at writing a story and see who can come up with the best one. So, they started competing; Charlotte, the elder sister, Emily, the middle sister and Anne, the younger sister. As for Branuel, their brother, he was handsome and very smart. He was the smartest among them and the most talented. Because of his gracefulness, women from the village were competing to seduce him, so he started drinking wine at an early age. Their sisters considered him their salvation, their savior from their tragic and sad life. But Branuel just continued living his life easy, staying up all night drinking with his lady friends and sleeping all morning. His tuberculosis, which he had like his mother, became worse. In the end, his choices became his death. His death came as a hard blow to the sisters who felt like they now lost their last hope at a good life.

Their tragedies just kept piling up, like layers forming on top of each other, so they escaped to the one thing that made them happy – writing stories. But they would never know that their stories, that were meant as an escape, would become pieces of literature that would change the world of literature and be taught all over the world.

Now let us look at the role played by each of the members in the family.

The Bronte Sisters: They are the center of the story (Charlotte, Emily, and Anne). They represent the core, which was characterized by the interactive and encouraging movement of the three sisters. The role of the Bronte Sisters represented the highest performance, movement, and cognitive product. All of them played that harmonious role of encouraging themselves and resisting their sadness and tragedy. They reflected the best example for women, the integrated cognitive construction, for their generation, the literary history, and the whole world.

The role of the father Patrick: His role reflected, since the earliest moments, his love and affection for his children, no matter the sacrifices. Moreover, he was smart enough to choose what to teach them, to help their imagination and talents to grow. He was really innovative in building their talents and opening windows into the world. Patrick exploded their imagination by stories, colors, tales, and playing music. Thus, their springs of inspiration, imagination, composition, construction, and configuration started.

The shocking role of the mother's death: Despite the shocking tragedy of their mother's death, the incident formed the motivation they needed to look for hope and salvation. Their imagination of their mother in line with the stories they read, and the tales they heard from the nanny, helped them in creating their own world, where they found their salvation. Despite the gloominess of this role, it played a significant role in creating their genius.

The nanny's role: The role of the nanny was integrated with the father's role in creating the imagination of the children. The nanny, with her distinctive way, was telling them simple tales, which inspire children's mind. The tales were about what was happening in the village and what the rich people of the village were doing in their lives, their fantasies, and their emotions. The stories also included amazing tales of love that showed the importance of sacrifice, nobility, and devotion. Thus, all of these had motivated their imagination, and had created a store of pictures, shapes, characters, and voices. This role complemented the father's role perfectly, and it filled their time with entertainment, education, and motivation. (In addition, we shall show the critical importance of tales and stories in forming cognitive construction of children at an early stage of their life).

The role of the elder sister Charlotte: Charlotte had a role that no one could perform other than her. She was one of them, the same age as them, and the one who understood their language, their dreams, and what they admired. Charlotte played her role with a natural instinct, making them compete in drawing, writing poetry and stories, and reading. They were writing together, drawing together on the same table, eating together and sleeping together. She infused them with the boldness to write stories and poetry and send them to magazines to publish under false men names (at this time it was not allowed for girls to write literature) and as a result they won cash prizes from those magazines.

The aunt's role: The aunt's role had positive and negative impacts. She was harsh to a point that terrified them. Her role was to allow them to trust her enough in matters that girls their age do not feel comfortable disclosing to anyone but their mother. She had to answer everything that confused them and help them find the peace, tenderness, and kindness that they were looking for. They had dreams like girls at their age do; thus, it was a smart and wise idea of their father to bring in their aunt to live with them. He knew that there was a role that he could not perform at this age. In spite of all this, they always felt she was their aunt, and she would never be their mother.

The shocking role of the brother: Branuel was like no one else, with a special place in the girl's hearts. They put all their hopes and wishes upon his shoulders; after all he was their only brother; handsome and smart, with his delicate sense which was reflected in his passion for drawing. However, he shocked them, and instead of being their savior from pain and bad circumstances, he was another blow in their already tragic lives. It was as if fate was telling them that they would never be happy even in their imagination, and whenever they felt happy, it must be followed by pain.

They were young but smart girls. They used their pain to create happiness, to fly away to another world and this reflected the secret of their genius.

If you wanted to use connectivity, reasoning, and verification, the story of the Bronte Sisters is similar to that of Steve Jobs. It was the gloomy, shocking, and bitter feeling of being an outcast child, whose parents had rejected from their lives that started the foundation of who the man he became. It was the largest motivation in Steve's life, and the day he came back to the company after leaving it, he became its volcano, medicine, and savior who saved it from the abyss. It was one of the main motivations of his genius, with all of its grades, as if he wanted to tell the whole world: I am Steve.

The same connection could be made with another genius who was also fueled by incidents in his childhood – Charles Darwin. Once, his father accused him of being a disgrace to the whole family. On one hand his grandfather was a scientist, a doctor, a poet, a philosopher, and a writer, and on the other, his father was a significant doctor in his community. Even his brother was teaching at the School of Medicine (Edinburgh), but Darwin was just a failure. In boarding school for seven years his results were below average, and even after going to Edinburgh University in the hopes of becoming like his brother, Darwin stayed two years in the same level and then failed. Instead of focusing on his studies, he preferred hunting, collecting insects, mice, and plants. Thus, the only option left for his father was to admit him into the School of Theology at Cambridge University to graduate as a priest and a theologian.

His father's disappointment was a great crush for Darwin, sensitive as he was. His father forgot that his mother's death at an early stage of Darwin's life made him heartbroken, and inside he was still the young and simple child who missed his mother sorely. He forgot that he missed her tenderness and warmth, and could not find it no matter how hard he looked. Darwin looked for his mother's lost love among his sisters but couldn't find a replacement for it. So, he decided to be by himself, which was why he loved nature and the solitude he found in it. This is the same Charles Darwin who made a scientific revolution when he published his book "The Origin of Species".

The next logical question to all these stories: Do we have to shock others with pain, adversities, and tragedies in order to emerge their genius and innovations and to construct their knowledge?

Hold on to this question as you read the next story and in it you will find the answer.

In 1890, Dr. William Coley was working as a doctor of orthopedic surgery at the New York Cancer Hospital, which later became the largest and oldest center specializing in the treatment and studies of cancer in the world (Memorial Sloan-Kettering Cancer Center). He failed in the treatment of a patient who was suffering from cancer, and this patient died. He was full of sadness and doubt as to why he could not find a treatment. He was later called for an emergency for a person suffering from a severe cancerous tumor. The patient had red skin fever disease, caused by a type of bacteria, and was extremely fevered. After a period of being put under close observation in intensive care, it was evident that this patient had fully recovered from cancer. The reason behind that was the bacteria that attacked him lead to a rise in his temperature. This type of bacteria attacked the cancer cells and destroyed it. His discovery was later recorded with his name "Coley toxins", and became a new treatment for cancer.

Dr. Coley's method did not have the expected success when other doctors started using it, which made them drop it quickly. Today doctors have come back to this method in the hope that further developing it could lead to its re-use with modern techniques. According to Time magazine they are aiming for it to become the "new hope" of the century for the treatment of cancer.[6]

Role of the environment and community in building the Cognitive Structure

The surrounding environment means the place where we and other creatures live and are affected by; distinguished by specific characteristics and topography. Community means all the different community classes: all the people living in the same area share cultural, civilizational, ideological, and legal characteristics. It also includes all the educational, health and security systems, organizations, and institutions that form

---

[6] http://www.thetimes.co.uk/tto/science/medicine/article3513692.ece Frances Hubbard- 21 August 2012- thetimes.co.uk –TIMEUK-© 2012 Times Newspapers Ltd.

this community and all what the individual needs for his communication and relationships.

None of the factors that affect building the cognitive structure (mind), can take the place of the environment and community factor, if they are absent and do not play their role in an integrated civilized way. The family, surrounding environment, and community factors are the most important factors affecting building the cognitive structure; in case of their absence or regression of their role, especially in the initial phases of one's life, it could lead to detrimental effects that would be difficult to treat. In such case the cognitive outcomes of the individual, even after reaching their maximum limits, will be less than the level required to build a civilization or international innovation, regardless of exceptional cases that can't be measured upon. The active existence of highly cultured families and a highly cultured environment guarantees to a certain extent a high level of cognitive outcome on the scale of individuals and community, provided that the active interaction of the integrated building persists for a long time.

Charles Darwin is the best example of the role played by the environment and community to achieve the highest integrated building of the cognitive structure. The integration and interaction of the environment and community produced the most amazing genius which raised controversy and became the main concern of opponents and proponents who either were alarmed at his findings or praised his genius.

Thomas S. Kuhn in his book "The Structure of Scientific Revolutions" (Chicago University -1962) wrote that what Darwin made is a model of the outcome of the scientific revolution, which isn't merely a scientific theory that results from the technological development, but it's more powerful and bold that produces new thinking approaches. Those approaches have led to a radical change in the basic concepts and old thinking methods and put them on equal foot with the revolution made by theories of Sir Isaac Newton when he published his book "Mathematical Principles of Natural Philosophy" which put an end to the dominance of the writings of the French philosopher René Descartes and his dualism quotes.

In 1996, the American anthropologist Frank Sollowy thought that Darwin's bold theory is more important than theories of Albert Einstein and has more effect than the theory of the astronomer Copernicus which overthrew the Aristotle philosophy and his theories on nature and universe. The famous linguist Noam Chomsky believed that the development of any nation is measured by its understanding of the Evolution Theory. The French biologist, Jacques Monod who won the Nobel prize in the sixties, believed that what's strange about Darwin's theory is that everyone thinks that they understand it, due to its simplicity and beauty, despite its complicated nature.

So, what was the role played by the environment and community that drove Charles Darwin to come up with such a magical theory, that surprised the whole world and raised controversy since he published it in his book "The Origin of the Species"? How is the interaction and movement of the environment and community qualified for building an integral cognitive structure that generates innovation and genius, build knowledge, and establish civilizations?

When we refer to scientific and community organizations or institutions, we don't literally mean the buildings, equipment, technological capabilities or budgets, but we mean the integrated, active, experienced, and persistent system. This system has deep roots over long epochs of civilization advanced on all scientific, literary, technical, and social levels in a highly integral and active movement that depended on the accurate scientific objectivity and the deep-rooted bases in the community. These institutions and organizations are models for that integration when their parts are completed and their rings are linked together; at this point the cognitive structure stabilizes in the place where it grows and produces its fruits. These institutions could be in the form of:

1. Church

2. Governmental institutions
3. Schools, institutes, and universities
4. Scientific missions
5. Scientific, literary and art societies
6. Scientific, art, and literary references
7. Scientific debates
8. Scientific, literary, and art clubs
9. Community associations
10. Museums

The church (religious institutions)
The role of religious institutions is integral in the advancement of cognitive movement regardless if they are proponents or opponents to such scientific cognitive movement due to their effects on a large number of people. In the case of Darwin, despite the fierce enmity and opposition, the Westminster church received his body and buried him amongst other great celebrities who were buried in that church such as John Herschel and Isaac Newton.

Governmental institutions
The best given example for the active interaction of governmental institutions is the smart role played by the government when the Beagle vessel of the British Royal Navy, was adapted as a survey vessel and took part in three expeditions. This was at a time when the Royal Navy was the most powerful in the world. On its second survey voyage (1831-1836) the young naturalist and clergyman, Charles Darwin, was on board. The captain of the ship then, Captain Robert Fitzroy, was very interested in science and geology and had a book by Charles Lyell, one of the finest geologists of his age, titled the Principles of Geology. He gave Darwin the first part of the book to study while accompanying him on his voyage. This book made a lot of questions rise in Darwin's mind: how did life start on earth? What is the actual age of geological periods? How did these rocks accumulate? How are they deposited? How were their layers formed? How did life develop slowly? Did species other than humankind develop according to the same mechanisms?

The search for the answers to all these questions led him to revolutionize science with the Evolution theory, and it all started with the role played with the governmental institution who decided not to waste one of its resources, the Beagle. Instead of letting it rust after doing what it was built for (celebrating the coronation of King George IV), they decided to further utilize it in a new avenue, and send it to out as a survey vessel.

Schools, institutes, and universities
Imagine that history stopped at the point when Dr. Robert Darwin blamed his son and told him how disappointed he was in him? Like him, there are many, with abilities and talents that society sees as unusable or unimportant and with that pressure, they kill their talents and try to become "normal", when instead they could have become "extraordinary" if only given some support and acceptance.

If we look at the kind of student Darwin was in his boarding school (Shrewsbury School), with his headmaster always complaining to his father about his carelessness and negligence, who could have anticipated the kind of future this boy would actually have? If we look further at his studies in the University of Edinburgh, his failure for two years would make most think of him as a disappointment with no hopes for a good future. But in fact, the university gave him a chance to know some of the best scientific minds of that time in a lot of different specializations. He came to know many famous scientists, amongst them the botanist Robert Edmond Grant who was the first professor holding a PhD degree in zoology and veterinary medicine.

We here emphasize that the integrated educational process shall never be limited to lectures, test, and academic degrees. The actual elements that are more important, and that most of the educational institutions miss out on, is the experience and the interactive relationship between teacher and student. These elements added a lot to Darwin's character.

If we are to look with scientific objectivity at most educational institutions, we would find that they miss the chance to appreciate and help grow many talents, abilities, and geniuses.

Even after his failure, Darwin's father still hoped to salvage something by admitting him to Cambridge to become a clergyman. In Cambridge, Darwin met his share of famous and great scientists, historians, politicians, economists, and writers. His dedicated, sincere, and honest efforts to have a better future might not have led to a scientific revolution if he hadn't been in a close contact with some of the greatest minds in the world. The most effective character in Darwin's life in that phase was the brilliant botanist John Stevens Henslow. John's intelligence, kindness, and wisdom attracted Darwin, and soon the two became close friends. They enjoyed long walks in the garden where they shared their passion for botany and zoology, among other things.

One day Darwin returned home to find a letter from his friend and mentor, John Henslow, nominating him for a five-year survey trip around the world aboard the Beagle. At first his father rejected the idea, considering it a waste of time, but was finally persuaded by relatives to let him travel after hearing about his scientific research abilities from his professors. Darwin, the confused young researcher, traveled to different places where he could broaden his cognitive horizons. During his journey, he used to correspond with brilliant scientists at Cambridge University and send samples and notes to the Natural History Museum, where an elite group of great and eminent scientists in different specialization analyzed his work. Through their collaborations and through the help of an active educational institution, the depressed young man whose father thought was a failure, became Charles Darwin the famous naturalist.

Scientific missions
The European expeditions that started in the fifteenth century travelled many known and unknown countries around the world, collecting samples and fossils of animals, insects, birds, and wood from ancient

ages. They studied, analyzed, classified, reviewed, evaluated, explained, and compared them through a deep, well-established, and continued scientific method under the supervision and sponsorship of expert scientists passionate about science and new discoveries for the sake of science. It was one of the most powerful and integrated scientific research periods throughout history.

If we look into the history of these expeditions we will see the following places were visited,

First: 1826 – 1830 to South America
Second: 1831 – 1836 to New Zealand and Australia with Charles Darwin on board
Third: 1837 – 1943 to Australia and the Timor Sea

Scientific, literary, and art societies

Scientific, literary, and art societies have a profound and dominant role that extends deeply in scientific history. Charles Darwin, for example, was a member of the Linnaean society named after the naturalist and founder of taxonomy, Carl Linnaeus. The society had a number of renowned scientists in their member list such as Charles Lyell, a well-known geologist and stratigraphist, and Joseph Dalton Hooker, the prominent botanist. Joseph Hooker was one of the great discoverers of the 19th century, who encouraged Charles Darwin to publish his theory when he hesitated, after the scientist Alfred Russel Wallace wrote a paper on the same subject that Darwin was tackling. Realizing that they had arrived at similar conclusions, the two scientists decided to co-author the paper.

The important thing to note here is the support and advocacy of the society members, who motivated Darwin to move forward with his life changing discoveries and publish it. This society helped shape his future and made him a renowned scientist. By the end of 1882, Darwin had become a member of 57 scientific societies.

Scientific, literary and art references
The role played by scientific magazines is complicated and continuous. Scientific magazines and references follow up regularly on every research, discovery, and new theory based on the well-established scientific fundamentals. There were various scientific journals that followed up on Darwin's theory since its emergence and published details not only about the theory, but also about his life. Amongst those, were the Biological Journal of Linnaean society, Geological Society, The North British Review, The Quarterly Review, The Nature (founded by Darwin in 1869), Edinburgh Magazine, and Earth Magazine, inter alia.

Scientific debates
Scientific debates that started with the unveiling of Darwin's theory, either pro or against, were based on either well established scientific or religious bases. During one of these debates, it was a surprise that Captain Robert Fitzroy, captain of the Beagle, who was a turning point in Darwin's life and scientific revolution, attended in support to The church's attitude. As a Christian, he was strictly committed to the holy book, yet after the debate he changed his mind.

In 1860, there was a debate in Oxford University, 7 months after Darwin's publication of his theory. Many renowned British scientists and philosophers attended, such as Thomas Henry Huxley, Samuel Wilber the bishop of Oxford, Joseph Dalton Hooker, the physiologist Benjamin Brodie, and Robert Fitzroy captain of Beagle. The attendees of this debate were not just there to spend a good time; they went to see how great minds think and argue their viewpoints.

Scientific, literary, and art clubs
Scientific, literary, and art clubs have played their entrusted role in continuing the movement of knowledge through connecting great minds together. An example of such a club is X club.

X club was formed in the late nineteenth century and included scientists who supported Darwin's theories like Thomas Henry Huxley, the

British biologist and anatomist, who initiated the formation of this club. All of the club members were of great scientific position and influence in the scientific British community. The nine members were:

- Thomas Henry Huxley: Comparative naturalist and anatomist
- George Pask: surgeon, old naturalist and biologist
- Edward Frankland: chemist
- Thomas Archer Hirst: specialist mathematician in geometry
- Joseph Dalton Hooker: botanist and one of Darwin's closest friends
- John Lubbock: encyclopedic botanist, biologist, entomologist, and archeologist
- Herbert Spencer: encyclopedic philosopher, biologist, socialist, and political liberalism theorist
- William Spotswood: mathematician and physicist
- John Nebtdal: physicist and chemist

After Darwin published his book "The Origin of Species", these scientists started working together to support the Naturalism issue. This collaboration of scientists, who were all part of the same scientific club, is but an example of the strength that can be obtained when great minds support each other and of the advancement that ensues such collaborations.

Community associations
Darwin was popular and loved for his kindness and friendliness. When an association was formed in his village (Dawn) that was affiliated to the church, he agreed to be a member regardless of his arguments with the church. This social interaction had a huge impact on Darwin's character and was one of the important means through which he was able to collect information about different plant and animals from people he worked and interacted with. This thus shows the important role the community can play in building the cognitive movement for individuals.

Museums

The British Museum for Natural History[7] is an example of a museum that played an efficient role in society, starting from collecting samples and excavations through non-stop research and exploration trips that was organized in coordination with universities and the British Royal Navy Fleet. In addition, following up these trips with accurate scientific planning, choosing the most genius minds in this field, analyzing, categorizing, and collecting notes regarding each specialty. Darwin's trip with the Beagle Ship, was an evidence for some of these events and the remarkable roles that were played by museums in an integral scientific trip. Here, a cognitive structure is being built and knowledge is being established to build up generations and to establish a civilization.

[7] http://www.tripadvisor.co.uk - /http://www.nhm.ac.uk

CHAPTER IV

In this chapter we will discuss:

1. The recent motivation to move towards knowledge and knowledge management
2. The illusion that data and information form knowledge
3. The first rule that governs cognitive construction
4. A realistic example on the illusion of data and information

The recent move towards knowledge and knowledge management

Knowledge management was founded as a modern science in the nineties. The founder of knowledge management, Nonaka, introduced this model in his book, which promoted this science, where he illustrates the main reasons for the superiority of the giant Japanese companies in the area of creativity.[8] Nonaka shows that the secret of the success of Japanese organizations such as Kao Kao, Honda, Canon, Sharp and NEC is a unique method adopted by organizations to manage and generate new knowledge. Led by these modern giants' technological figures, western countries moved towards this intellectual capital science to create a competitive advantage that would lead to the achievements of more market benefits and shares. Research and literature studies of knowledge management accelerated and generated many new branches of research in the same area. There was an agreement that it is a branch of science that could change resources into knowledge assets, financial capital into intellectual capital and the methods of efficiency and productivity into standards of value creation.

These are a few of the conclusions that research and study of the market has concluded:

1. Knowledge has become an asset with top marginal returns in comparison to all other assets. This is proved by the study of P.Strasmann when he accumulated the knowledge capital of Microsoft Corp., estimated to range between 67 and 91.6 billion dollars.[9]

---

[8] Nonak, Ikujiro and Takeuchi, Hirotaka (1995) The Knowledge Creating Company : How Japanese Companies Create the Dynamics of Innovation, New York, Oxford university Press

[9] Housel, Thomas and Bell, A. H. (2001) : Measuring and Managing Knowledge, McGraw-Hill/Irwin, Boston,p24

2. Knowledge management since the beginning of the late nineties became an ongoing project for all companies. [10]
3. Organizations have been increasingly concerned with knowledge management as a way to create a value. [11]
4. Knowledge management has increased the financial value of the organization, where the knowledge of individuals has become an asset. [12]
5. Knowledge management is a systematic process functioned to establish, care for, and maintain the organization. The aim is to achieve the best use of its knowledge on the individual and collective levels, and to achieve the organization's mission and objectives to reach the sustainable competitive advantage and high performance. [13]
6. The emergence of the new economy and the unique value of knowledge since it became their inexhaustible strategic resource and source of wealth. [14]
7. Knowledge management has caused a growing consensus that the capital of knowledge is critical to the success of companies and organizations. [15]

---

[10] Nonaka, Ikujiro (1991):The Knowledge-Creating Company,HBR, Vol(68), No.(6), Nov-Dec,pp96-104.

[11] De Brùn, C. (2005), **ABC of Knowledge Management,** NHS National Library for Health: Specialist Library Knowledge Management.

[12] Cong, X. and Pandya, K. (2003), **Issues of Knowledge Management in the Public Sector,** Electronic Journal of Knowledge Management, Vol. 1, Issue 2, p.p. 25-33.

[13] Bennet, A. and Bennet, D. (2003), **The Partnership between Organizational Learning and Knowledge Management,** In: Holsapple, W. *Handbook on Knowledge Management: Knowledge Matters*, New York: Springer-Verlag, Chapter 23, p.p. 439-455.

[14] Toffler A., (1990), Power Shift: Knowledge, Wealth and Violence at the Edge of the 21st Century, Bantam Books, New York.

[15] Yusliza Mohd.Yusoff, Hazman Shah Abdullah, Managing Human Capital in a Knowledge Based Economy: The Role of the HR Function, Proceedings of the Knowledge Management International Conference: Transferring, Managing and Maintaining Knowledge for Nation Capacity Development, Langkawi, Malaysia, 10-12 June, 2008.

8. Intellectual resources management through knowledge management has become one of the most important functions of government, businesses, and individuals in contemporary society. [16]

9. On the international level, knowledge has become one of the most important factors in economic growth and competitive advantage. [17]

10. Knowledge is the launching pad for all directors who seek to focus their companies and organizations around employees and their success, and the achievement of competitive advantage. [18]

11. We are entering into a society where knowledge forms the basic economic resource and can be turned into capital composed of intangible assets, which are not apparent in the budget and which includes the employee skills, knowledge, intellectual property, and use the use of innovative assets. [19]

12. Knowledge is considered as a source of sustainable competitive value since it contributes in identifying strategic capacities. [20]

13. The successful experience of knowledge management applications implemented by IBM Global Services has fulfilled as increase of 400% in the service revenues.[21]

---

[16] Claudia Sarrocco, intellectual capital in the information society, available at: http://www.itu.int/visions, (14/03/2012(

[17] Whicker, L.M and Andrews, K. M, HRM in the Knowledge Economy: Realising the Potential, Asia Pacific Journal of Human Resources, V42, N2, 2004.

[18] Paul Squires, concept paper on managing human capital, available at: http://www.appliedskills.com/White%20Papers/Human_Capital.pdf, (27/03/2013).

[19] Drucker P., (1995): "**The Information executive truly need**", Harvard Business Review, Jan-Feb.

[20] *Tarondeau J.C. Le Management Des Savoirs, Paris : PUF,1998, P05. Ikujiro Nonaka and N.Konno*

[21] Wesley Vestal (2002): *Measuring Knowledge Management,* from: http: //www.providersedge.com/ docs/km_articles/measuring_km.pdf, Access date, 12012/9/.

The illusion that data and information form knowledge

Many scientists dealt with knowledge from the standpoint that it was only data and information. The formed their famous equation based on this conjecture, which was:

Data + Information = Knowledge   X

Based on this equation, they built many other equations[22] and figures[23], [24]. Owing to this, many concepts overlapped to provide the meaning of knowledge, and as a result this affected all the processes of cognitive restructuring in many countries. A five-year study by Fahey and Prusak,[25] which was conducted on one hundred knowledge projects, has shown that many directors of such projects do not prefer using the term knowledge and that they prefer dealing with the terms data and information instead.

But is this knowledge? Can we reach excellence with just data and information? Can this be the reason for innovation? Can this increase benefits and capital? **Knowledge and the integrated cognitive construction are far greater than the issue of just data and information.**

---

[22] Methodology An Empirical Approach in Core Sectors in ESCWA Member Countries ", New York, (2003)United Nations Economic and Social Commission for Western Asia ESCWA," Knowledge Management

[23] Jonathan Hey, the Data, Information, Knowledge, Wisdom Chain: The Metaphorical link, available at:
http://www.dataschemata.com/uploads/7/4/8/7/7487334/dikwchain.pdf, (22/02/2013), p02.

[24] Martin Frické, The Knowledge Pyramid: A Critique of the DIKW Hierarchy, Journal of Information Science, available at: http://jis.sagepub.co.uk, (25/03/2013).

[25] Fahey, L. and Pursak, L. (1998) : The Eleven Deadly Sins of Knowledge Management, California, Management Review, Vol.(40), No.(3), Spring, p268.

> The first rule in cognitive construction
>
> Data + Information ≠ **Knowledge**
>
> Knowledge is greater than all that is based on this equation

It is urgent to reach the right identification of the concept of knowledge and review what has been based on this concept. Unless we understand the reality and components of knowledge we will not be able to manage or invest it. How can we deal with something that is ambiguous to us? We understand the interest in knowledge, and as such it is not just a theoretical or even philosophical topic, but a modern-day question that needs answering.

So, is it a practice or is it an experience, or both?

By applying the same approach on which we based our method in dealing with data and information we can understand why others think so. We do not deal with any subject on the basis that one part or many parts is/are the whole part(s). This is not the right method if we desire to reach an integrated sense. Although information, data, science, understanding, practice, and experience are individually or collectively important in the formation of knowledge, all or any of these cannot form knowledge.

Therefore, the following equation cannot be accepted:

Information + data + science + understanding + practice + experience= knowledge X

What is the value of the parts of the car individually or collectively without the engine and fuel? Can you call such parts a car by themselves?

Surely knowledge is not composed of science alone which you can learn or review through a book, course, workshop or any means of social media. The same applies to data and information, experience and the other parts that contribute either directly or indirectly to the formation of cognitive restructuring. This narrow view of knowledge resulted in limiting the identification of knowledge to items which cannot be independently called knowledge. Due to this, we considered the installation and dismantling of a machine to be knowledge, that understanding the procedures and rules of work as knowledge, and learning something which has been neglected as knowledge. As a result of this approach the item "knowledge" has been surrounded with confusion and ambiguity. This has further resulted in many hastening the process of cognitive restructuring and waiting for its fruits, which even when produced, were worthless.[26]

Scientists, researchers and persons who are concerned with knowledge disagreed on knowledge in terms of terminology. The following are a few of their definitions:

- Know-how[27] (procedural knowledge) - This relates to the technical know-how, how things work, how to dismantle, assemble, and deal with a machine, how to insert data, and knowing the different procedures.
- Know-what (cognitive knowledge) - This is further than know-how because it relates to reaching the highest level of experience about a subject.
- Know-why – This requires knowing the rules and relations between things. It includes a deep knowledge of relations and decision making.
- Know-who - This relates to knowing who is responsible for knowledge in general in terms of content, method and purpose.

---

[26] Hislop, Donald (2005). Knowledge Management in Organizations: A Critical Introduction. Oxford: Oxford University Press.
[27] Kathryn A. B & G. M. Badamshina (2004):Knowledge Management, 2 / e, New York, Idea Grouo Publishing

There have been more names such as deep knowledge, innovative knowledge, shallow knowledge, knowledge-oriented, advanced knowledge, core knowledge, and other titles and divisions. The vast majority of scientists including the founding fathers of the modern science of knowledge tended to divide knowledge into two divisions:

1. Tacit Knowledge: This is the hidden or concealed knowledge. It is considered the origin of knowledge and its building. It is made up in the mind of its owner, and is hidden from others, perhaps hidden from that same owner in terms of composition and structure.
2. Explicit Knowledge: This is clear, declared, written, or explicit knowledge. Knowledge becomes explicit once it comes out of the mind of its maker and is recorded, published, written, announced, and accessible.

A realistic example on the illusion of information and data

To better illustrate what knowledge is, we are going to look at the examples of 2 different carpenters at opposite sides of the world: one in an African village and the other at a Chinese village.

The two men have been working as carpenters for fifteen years. Both learned carpentry at a specialty school, where they spent the same number of years studying and learning. They both had almost the same amount of experience. They were only different in terms of family, country, community, environment, and lifestyle.

Based on the story so far, what are the cognitive components of each of them?

1. Both of them have almost equal educational degrees in carpentry.
2. Both have theoretical and practical understanding about carpentry in terms of work, materials, tools, fittings, and designs.

3. Both have hands-on training, practice, and 15-year-experience

The question then: Do they both have knowledge?

Based on the studies, research, and literature in the science of knowledge, both of them have knowledge. Scientists would agree on that they both have the fundamentals of knowledge; however, they would probably disagree on the details.

Most scientists and researchers would agree that each of them has tacit knowledge, and the first founding scientists of modern science of knowledge such as Polanyi, Nonaka, and Takayoshi would agree to that. Tacit knowledge here, according to scientists, means what they both learned, exclusively, through the educational process, training, practice, and experience. It thus becomes a component in their minds. This is tacit knowledge. [28, 29]

Some would differ and say that they both have know-how whereas others would say that they have know-what only

Let's go ahead with the story and try to come up with our own analysis.

The first carpenter
The first carpenter did not progress much in his work. He was lazy and did not want to put much effort in his work. He was not ambitious and was satisfied with his income. He was introverted and lacked the desire to renew his methods and research new methods. The first carpenter was not very fond of working. The only significant change he did was replacing his hand tools by electric tools, and only because they

---

[28] Wilson, Tom. (2002). The Nonsense of 'Knowledge Management' Information Research, 8:1- Stnamark sees that the knowledge of all kinds is tacit knowledge, and that information is explicit knowledge.

[29] Stenmark, D. (2001). "Leverage Tacit Organizational Knowledge", *Journal of Management Information Systems*, 17 (1). 9-24.(- Stenmark, D. (2001). "Leverage Tacit Organizational Knowledge", *Journal of Management Information Systems*, 17 (1). 9-24.(

became widespread, were cheap, and made his work easier. His outputs remained traditional without any change for fifteen years.

The second carpenter
The second carpenter had a passion for his work and a creative imagination. He was always thinking, learning, and constantly researching new methods. He had a stubborn mind, an unlimited ambition and a dream to become a pioneer in his field. He enjoyed showing off his technical capabilities in his wood adaptations and artistic designs; however, this was not enough to attain his ambition. He wanted more and more achievements. His progress was unlimited. One day, he read that a carpenter in one of the neighboring countries made a bicycle from wood, start to end. Reading that, he became determined to make a wooden car that would run on electrical energy. He became driven, working endless hours without respite. His determination, desire, ambition, mobility, research, and constant drive were all the kinetics of cognitive training.

So, does ambition, movement, initiative, and determination generate new energy in a person? Yes!

Ask yourself this, why do you feel happy when you achieve our goals, no matter what they are, or how small or big? Why do we feel excited when we solve a hard mathematics problem? Why do we feel like we are happier or have more energy when we listen to a song we love? Why do we not feel tired when we are doing work that pleases us, no matter the obstacles we face?

The second carpenter raced against time, and every challenge he faced only succeeded in increasing his enthusiasm and determination, providing him with even more energy.

How is such determination and energy generated? Does this ambition and drive make new cells in the brain so as to give the body the push and energy it requires to reach its goal? Or, is it only caused by data, information, practice, and experience?

To succeed he needed to have both! This is how knowledge is made and this is how it manifests itself.

So where is the second carpenter now?

He succeeded in fulfilling his ambition and making a wooden car that runs on electrical energy. Here, the cognitive restructuring process is made, talents and skills develop, and mental and nerve cells become active, just as it happened to Michael when his knowledge store generated new knowledge resulting from reading events, picking up the signals, and sensing what's going to happen. Only then was he successful in making a decision to save his team. When he moved, thought, drew comparisons, and contemplated enough, his knowledge components interacted to produce a new method in decision making at a time of crisis, taking quick action, and intervening rapidly.

So, lets analyze the story of the two carpenters:

1. Are they equal?
2. Taking tacit knowledge into account, that scientists would agree they both have, can we claim that they both have the same level of knowledge?
3. If both are employed within a company, which one would add more benefit to the company and himself in the process?
4. Which one would be considered intellectual capital for the company and reliable in terms of competition?
5. Has the first carpenter added anything to the field of carpentry? Has his alleged knowledge produced anything?
6. What will the first carpenter versus the second carpenter convey to others?

7. If the first carpenter was to work in a company, will the knowledge stores of the company increase and as a result the company would compete better?
8. Where will the second carpenter reach with his learning, practice, experience, development, interactivity, thought, meditation, research, imagination, and dynamicity? This is knowledge.

So, can we now say with confidence:

$$\text{Data + information= knowledge} \qquad \textbf{X wrong}$$

Also, that:

$$\text{Data + information+ experience + understanding+ learning= knowledge} \qquad \textbf{X wrong}$$

As well as:

$$\text{Data + information+ experience + understanding+ learning x participation= knowledge}$$
$$\textbf{X wrong}$$

So, the question is, how will scientists classify the knowledge formed in the minds of the two carpenters after taking into consideration their cognitive inputs and outputs?

Most scientists would agree:

1. The two carpenters have the know-how, i.e. they have the technical knowledge about carpentry and have to create wooden structures
2. Some scientists may define the knowledge of the first carpenter as shallow knowledge
3. All scientists will agree that both carpenters have tacit knowledge, i.e., the knowledge components required for the carpentry.

4. They will agree that the second carpenter has deep knowledge, and some would say he is innovative and has advanced or deep knowledge

Anyway, according to the literature, theories, and the advanced research done in the field of modern science of knowledge even by the founding fathers, there is almost a consensus on:

1. The two carpenters have knowledge
2. Both carpenters at least have tacit knowledge

The problem is not based on the term used to refer to knowledge. It is based, in my opinion, on the non-integrated confused cognitive restructuring based on this term. This, we will try to further elaborate on in the following chapters.

CHAPTER V

In this chapter we will discuss:

- Tacit and explicit knowledge
- How did tacit knowledge originate?

Tacit and explicit knowledge

We will present here tacit and explicit knowledge from the perspective of their respective scholars and we will discuss each thoroughly.

Is the formation and emergence of knowledge tacit (i.e. does it stem from inside an individual)?

The Hungarian scientist and philosopher Michael Polanyi, in 1966, was the first to speak about the principles of knowledge, its formation, and research deeply its principles. His supporters conveyed and learnt from his results the reality of knowledge, its origins, principles, formation, and reference. Among them were the Japanese scientists Nonaka and Takuchi, who carried out significant research on knowledge and its enrichment. Their work was approved and acknowledged by world scientific authorities and references.

How did tacit knowledge originate?

What does tacit knowledge mean?

First, let's try to describe knowledge. It is what an individual knows of different theoretical, or applied sciences, techniques, or methods, etc. that he did not previously know, and thus for him this is knowledge.

Second, let's review what tacit knowledge is. Tacit is a description of knowledge that forms inside one's mind (cognitive organ), hence it's personal in terms of origin, formation, and production. It is hidden in one's mind, not only from others, but sometimes from himself as well. It is built through interactions, images, concepts, situations, readings, and practices. Some of them have been formed over a long time and others have been formed in a short time. So, one's past, and present are mixed, compiled, connected, and composed to produce knowledge.

This is what lead Polanyi to say that personal knowledge is individual in its origin and formation. This is important to note as many significant cognitive principles are based on this idea.

The knowledge that Newton produced is the outcome of the life he lived; therefore it's an individual personal knowledge. The knowledge that Einstein produced is the outcome of the life he lived. The knowledge that Michael produced is the outcome of his reasoning, contemplation, imagination, readings, experiences, and practices which interacted forming what is called knowledge. Therefore, it's an individual personal knowledge. The knowledge that originates of forms is externalized from the person. If one does not disclose it, it remains hidden in the mind, hence it is called tacit. This happened with Michael when he was asked, what made him make a decision to take his team out quickly and he replied that he could not say any specific reason- it was just a feeling of discomfort and worry. He saw signs that were not similar to anything he has seen before and that inspired him to make that decision. The next logical question then, is whether when tacit knowledge is externalized, is it externalized fully, i.e., do all of its components externalize or is it just a small part of it? Proponents of tacit and explicit knowledge would explain that what is externalized is like the part of the iceberg that shows on the surface; a very small part of the actual iceberg (**figure 10**).

Figure 10: Tacit and explicit knowledge

"We know more than we can tell and perhaps we have no ability to tell others how we do"
(Michael Polanyi) [30]

This is true when this newborn knowledge is externalized: it's only a small part of the long complicated compiled cognitive fusion that spread its strings in the mind, weaving fibers and layers and forming sediments and spectra.

But, whoever looks deeply at tacit knowledge will understand that when it is produced it is called expressed knowledge. In this way, there is no difference between tacit and explicit knowledge. However, this is in opposition of what others have believed, that externalized knowledge is a small part of tacit knowledge.

---

[30] PERSONAL KNOWLEDGE - MICHAEL Towards a Post-Critical Philosophy POLANYI Psychology Press, 1998.

They call it knowledge during its formation and production, which cannot be. If its knowledge when its forms, and also knowledge when produced and externalized, what is the difference?

To understand this better, imagine the development of a human from a sperm and an egg to a fetus. Is it a fetus both as it is being formed and as it is born? What about the embryo? If you plant a seed, is it a seed as it is formed, and as it grows into a tree? In the same way with knowledge, how do we understand its origin, composition, formation, and its phases? How can we form it without knowing its origins? And can the origins also be called knowledge?

It's knowledge when it's produced but when being formed it's something else. It's knowledge for those who produce it; however, it's something else for those who study and comprehend the Stem Cells Cognitive Theory (SCC) which we will clarify later.

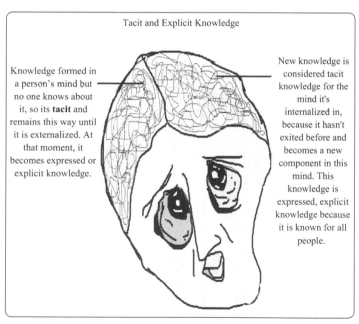

Tacit and Explicit Knowledge

Knowledge formed in a person's mind but no one knows about it, so its **tacit** and remains this way until it is externalized. At that moment, it becomes expressed or explicit knowledge.

New knowledge is considered tacit knowledge for the mind it's internalized in, because it hasn't exited before and becomes a new component in this mind. This knowledge is expressed, explicit knowledge because it is known for all people.

Figure 11: Tacit and explicit knowledge
from the perspective of scholars

The division of knowledge into two parts, the hidden part "tacit" and the apparent part "explicit or expressed", is hasty and improper as it doesn't care for the cognitive formation and the long, complicated, and overlapped process of knowledge formation. This led to the emergence of spiral knowledge by Nonaka and Takuchi. Knowledge starts out tacit, then is externalized so it becomes explicit. In this stage, it is learnt by others who have not known it before, and thus becomes tacit knowledge for them as they take it in and build on it. They add more to that knowledge, increasing it, making it more complicated, and more developed which as a result forms tacit knowledge again which is then externalized and becomes explicit and so on. This is the base upon which Nonaka & Takuchi founded the SECI model. Furthermore, this is how knowledge is cycling in a spiral way from tacit to explicit knowledge and vice versa.

CHAPTER VI

We will discuss in this chapter:
- Knowledge hierarchy
- Data.
- Information.
- Knowledge hierarchical error analysis
- The Second rule in cognitive construction

Knowledge hierarchy

The expression knowledge hierarchy, along with the terms data and information, are frequently used in most scientific researches and publications that deal with knowledge and knowledge management in the modern age. One of the reasons behind this is the rapid development of the technological approach, whose subjects are data and information. Most parts of the cognitive structure, unless whole, are processed through dealing with data and information. Before we get any further, we should understand what is meant by data and information.

Data:
Suppose that you have a hardcopy or softcopy registry in which you register the names of your customers or patients. This registry, whatever its form, is a mean to present data. However, it is meaningless when mixed with other random data. If it isn't explained, clarified, compared or analyzed it remains raw material from which we can extract important information if we only add to it more details.

Information:
If we take, for example, one of the data lists of customer names and order them according to their importance and cooperation strength with the organization, we could end with a list where we see that 10 customers represent 90% of the company's income and the other 90 customers represent the rest of the company's income. From this list, we can conclude that the company can focus on those customers because they are the main source of its income or maybe the company uses these results to focus more on the rest of the customers to strengthen their cooperation and therefore the company won't be dependent only on ten percent of customers. The more the data is explained, analyzed, and compared with previous years or competitors or different products, the more results can be reached and the more meaning this data can have. As a result of this analysis, plans and decisions are made. This is information.

So to reiterate: data is the raw material, and if it's interpreted, explained and compared, it becomes information.

Knowledge hierarchical error analysis

As we mentioned before, due to the rapid development of technology, most people have thought that knowledge is the result of the equation:

Data + Information = Knowledge   **X Error**

or

Information + (Technology * Sharing Amount)
= Knowledge [31]   **X Error**
$$K = I + (T^\wedge S)$$

K = Knowledge
I = Information
T = Technology
S = Sharing amount (sharing of individuals specialized in data and information)

Meaning that data and information when processed by technological devices through sharing of all relevant parties, produce valuable knowledge. The more the sharing amount is increased(S), the higher, more valuable, and creative the results that can be reached are, and the more success we can achieve competing others. This is the main concern of large companies, and the main reason behind their successes that enables them to have bigger market shares and accordingly make more profit.

If we put data at the base of the pyramid, and we process it through comparisons, explanations, and ordering, it turns to information. If

[31] United Nations Economic and Social Commission for Western Asia ESCWA," Knowledge Management Methodology An Empirical Approach in Core Sectors in ESCWA Member Countries ", New York, (2003)

this information is further processed by reasoning, association, and deduction, we may come to a decision that serves the target (knowledge). If this cognitive process (producing knowledge) is being practiced for a long time gaining experience, understanding challenges and facing them, it becomes wisdom.

Therefore, we obtain cognitive hierarchy. Scholars have differed on what should be placed at the top of the pyramid. Some were of the opinion that it should be wisdom, while others saw that it should be experience, ability and intelligence.

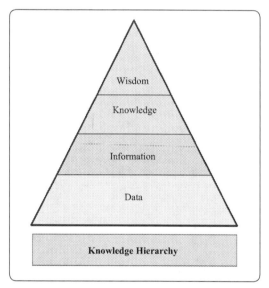

Figure 12: Knowledge hierarchy

Some scholars combined between information and knowledge, claiming that they are similar in some respects but differ in others. [32] Others were proponents of the opinion that knowledge hierarchy ascended from data, information, knowledge then wisdom.[33]

---

[32] Kogul, B & Zander, U. (1992). "Knowledge of the Firm: Combinative Capabilities and the Replication of Technology", Organization Science, 3 (2). 383-397.
[33] Stenmark, D. (2001). "Leverage Tacit Organizational Knowledge", *Journal of Management Information Systems*, 17 (1). 9-24.

Tuomi, in 1999, differed completely from others in his opinion concerning the relationship between these terms – data, information, and knowledge.

He emphasized that data is produced only when we have knowledge. He called for the rearrangement of the previous hierarchy which he called traditional. He presented the reversed hierarchy, saying that there cannot be derivations deduced from simple facts (referring to data) unless an individual produces it through using knowledge.[34]

The pyramid of knowledge model, developed by Raddad & Alan, show that the raw data and the implicit data form the base of the pyramid.[35]

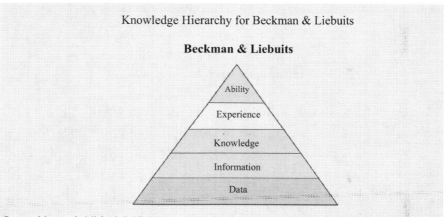

Knowledge Hierarchy for Beckman & Liebuits

Beckman & Liebuits

Ability
Experience
Knowledge
Information
Data

Source: Marquardt, Michael, J. " Building the Learning Organization: Mastering the 5Elements of Corporate Learning", U.S.A. Davis-Black publishing Company, 2002: 23

Figure 13: The Liebuits and Beckman
Knowledge Hierarchy

[34] El Kebiesy, Salah El Deen, Knowledge management. **Cairo**, Arab Administrative Development Organization, 2005.
[35] Coakes, Elayne (2003): "**Knowledge Management**", Current Issues and challenges, Idea Group Publishing: U.S.A.

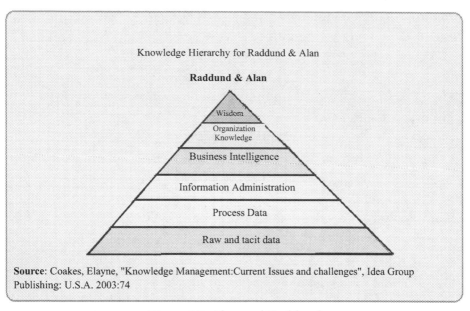

Knowledge Hierarchy for Raddund & Alan

Raddund & Alan

Wisdom
Organization Knowledge
Business Intelligence
Information Administration
Process Data
Raw and tacit data

Source: Coakes, Elayne, "Knowledge Management:Current Issues and challenges", Idea Group Publishing: U.S.A. 2003:74

Figure 13: Alan and Raddund
Knowledge Hierarchy Pyramid

Charles Dickens, British writer and one of the greatest writers in history, next to Shakespeare, used to hide in a small room in the upper floor, at the age of seven, and read stories like Don Quixote, Robinson Crusoe, and One Thousand and One Nights. Many people regard that as the secret behind the start of Dicken's genius, his fame, and his success.

But to conclude from this story this equation:

Reading books + Stories + Literature = Genius
writer or narrator **X Error**

If the above equation was true, why is it then that great scientists, interested in literature, who had the same circumstances, environment and conditions, and who were provided with data and information, did not come up with the same result or end up as famous as Dickens. There must be another way to look at this then. So, which equation should we write? Which knowledge pyramid shall we ascribe to this?

No equation can describe how Beethoven, the smartest musician of his age, produced his masterpieces, the fifth, sixth, and the ninth symphonies in his severe deafness? How could he listen to his own music? Did he listen to it in his mind? Did his imagination, suffering, eagerness, and painful joy help him? Was him mind creating and listening to these symphonies before their composition? Do we have senses other than those discovered by science and scientists? Can you hear, smell or see something just through imagining it?

Let's try to find the answer in David Frost's interview with Richard Nixon. He thought that he could trick him and prove what lawyers and trials couldn't, concerning the scandal of Watergate that was the reason of his downfall. David asked various channels and producers to bear the costs of that interview, which was going to be around two million dollars. No one agreed to take such risk, believing that no one would be able to prove such a thing against Nixon. David worried about the interview and was hesitant after he had already called Nixon's office and had initial approval. But Frost never quit: he decided to help financially fund the interviews himself. Additionally, he appointed a number of clever investigators and journalists. But after the first 3 episodes of the interview, by all accounts Nixon was successful in improving his public image and Frost was nowhere near his goal. There was panic amongst the production team.

Then it was time for the fourth and final episode. In a last gamble, David gave it his all and was able to make Nixon admit to his role in the Watergate scandal. So how did it happen? How was he able to do what no lawyer, judge or journalist could do?

To take data and information, then put them into equations and hierarchal and non-hierarchal figures, in order to accurately describe and analyze them, requires great accuracy, review, and patience.

We need to find the real roots of the cognitive structure, its correct formation, and movement. Knowledge is deeper, profounder, and of stronger structure, production, and origin. It's more eloquent and splendid than any other imagined structure or frame.

> Second rule of cognitive construction
>
> Knowledge cannot be put into any equation or frame, because limits for knowledge mean limits for creativity, and creativity should never be limited. All kinds of knowledge hierarchal forms weaken the value of knowledge and distort its meaning, structure, formation, and value.

CHAPTER VII

In this chapter:

- Knowledge Spiral Model (SECI model) according to Nonaka and Takeuchi.
- The aims that the knowledge SECI model focuses on.
- Work tools according to knowledge model (SECI model).
- The meaning of knowledge spiral.
- The existential dimension of knowledge according to knowledge spiral model (SECI model).
- The existential and cognitive dimension of knowledge according to knowledge spiral model (SECI model).
- How does the cognitive spatial helical movement occur?
- Detailing the four phases for knowledge spiral model (SECI model).
- Showing knowledge spiral model (SECI model) in points.

Knowledge Spiral Model (SECI model)

The Knowledge Spiral Model (SECI Model) of cognitive structuring for Nonaka & Takuchi[36] is considered as one of the best models which elaborates and details the cognitive structuring processes, as well as being the closest one to practical application.

This model has been admired and given credit to by international scientific organizations, as well as having the approval and support of global business companies. The Wall Street magazine described it in 2008 as the best thing provided in the field of knowledge management, whereas Takuchi was nominated as one of the greatest thinkers in the field of business. Nonaka also has similar fame, admiration, and appreciation, having been described by Business Week magazine as one of the greatest ten thinkers in the field of management and business.

So, what do these letters "SECI" refer to?

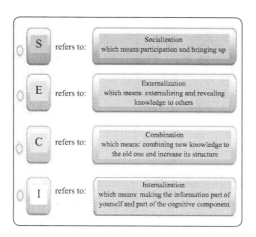

---

[36] Nonaka, I. (1994). "A Dynamic Theory of Organizational Knowledge Creation", *Organization Science*, 5 (1). 14-37.

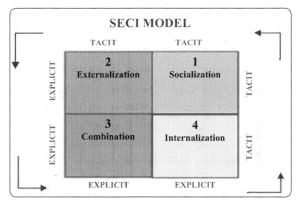

Figure 14: The SECI Model

Figure 14 shows two different depictions of the SECI model used by Nonaka & Takuchi to show the working of this model.

What are the aims which SECI model focuses on?

The first and most important aim of the SECI model is to activate the collective cognitive creation mechanisms. This would result in creating creative based companies that are based on knowledge, which would thus increase the competitive advantage via sharing knowledge and expanding its space. This happens through four phases as shown by figure 14. It starts with the individual (individual tacit), that presents their knowledge to the group, who in turn shares the development of this knowledge on a bigger scale. Accordingly, the configuration process moves from the individual tacit to the collective tacit, represented by the first phase of participation (**socialization**) which prepares for the second phase.

Second phase (externalization): This occurs via externalizing the cognitive newborn and moving it from the tacit to the explicit phase, where it is worked, applied, and published in a limited scope, preparing it for the third phase.

Third phase (combination): The cognitive newborn moves via the initial application to more complex and complicated forms, where it is combined with other forms or old knowledge, as it is circulated around the company or the organization as a whole.

Fourth phase (internalization): The fourth phase results in a new cognitive component for the whole organization, through the publishing, documenting, recording, and archiving process that makes it available to all. As Nonaka[1] asserts in his SECI Model of the cognitive structure: the aim of the cognitive structuring processes is to create new knowledge.

This is the main reason and the essence of creating and establishing the subject of knowledge and knowledge management in the modern age; it stems from business companies desiring to achieve a competitive advantage through creation processes which are generated from knowledge.

Knowledge is the engine of creativity, its creator, sponsor and womb; there is no creativity without knowledge and there is no worth or value for knowledge that we keep, store, sort or publish unless it generates creativity and adds new avenues.

---

1.   Nonaka, Ikujiro (1998) The Knowledge – Creating Company, Harvard Business Review on Knowledge Management, U.S.A., Harvard Business

Work tools of the SECI model

The work tools of this model are based on the interaction between tacit and explicit knowledge, which is in a rising, increasing, and growing (spiral) movement.

Knowledge commences from the individual, and so accordingly, the creation process of knowledge that companies target, from stem to stern, is based on the individual. The role of the organization here is considered as the backbone, to make this structure work and achieve the targeted results.

What is the meaning of spiral knowledge?

It means that there are two dimensions for knowledge, between tacit knowledge (which stems from the individual) and explicit knowledge (which occurs within the group). Taking this knowledge within an organization as a whole, then all organizations, and finally the whole world, this cognitive interaction process takes in the perception of spiral shape that allows for the increase in knowledge and spreads it continuously.

The first dimension for knowledge is the cognitive, which means creating and forming knowledge.[37] As we have identified previously, knowledge stems in its first stage from the individual, as it is still in the tacit phase. As soon as it's externalized from the individual's mind to meet the ideas of others through discussions, work seminars etc., this knowledge starts to be mixed with the ideas of others, then increases and spreads through laws, procedures, ways, and new methods. This is the phase in which knowledge becomes explicit (according to the theory).

---

[37] **Phatak, A.V. & Bhagat**, R.S. & Kashlak, R.J. (2005) International Management. McGraw: Boston.

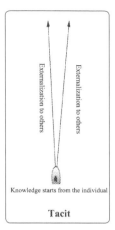

Figure 15: Tacit knowledge starting from an
individual and externalizing to the outer world.

As seen in **figure 15**, you can imagine that the first dimension goes
in a vertical direction from the first point in which knowledge forms
and creates in the individual's mind, then directs up towards the group
and individual, to be discussed, reviewed and met with the ideas of
the others. As soon as it is externalized to others and spreads, it can be
depicted as seen in **figure 16**.

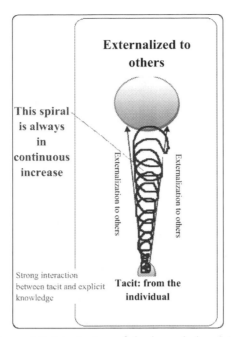

Figure 16: Depiction of the knowledge spiral

The second dimension of knowledge is the existential dimension, which is the existence of knowledge and its spread. This dimension takes into account the way knowledge spreads from an individual to a group and later to an organization as a whole, and finally the rest of the organization where anyone can benefit from it, review it, and understand it. This dimension is represented as follows:

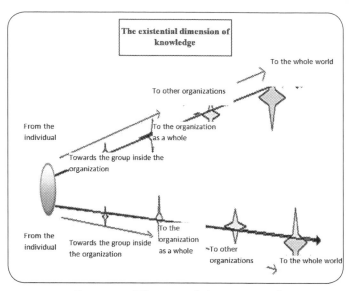

Figure 17: The second dimension of knowledge – the existential dimension

If we took into account the knowledge spiral, then the true depiction will be as seen in **figure 18**.

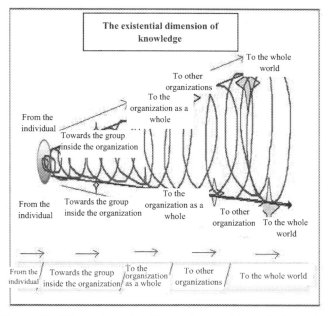

Figure 18: The existential dimension and knowledge spiral

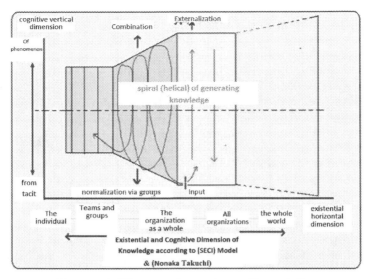

Figure 19: The two dimensions of knowledge
according to the SECI Model

Figure 19 shows the final output of the interaction between the two dimensions of knowledge, including the knowledge spiral and the phases of the SECI model.[38]

So, how does the cognitive spiral movement, through the cognitive dimension and existential dimension, occur to reach an international spread.

Nonaka & Takuchi have detailed this spiral interaction which occurs between tacit and explicit knowledge through four main phases

Detailing the four phases to SECI model

First phase - socialization: sharing and bringing up.

The tacit knowledge phase, which consists in the mind of the individual, is promoted in this phase to a new more active, expressive, and descriptive

---

[38] Nonaka m Ikujiro & Takeuchi, Hirotaka. "Hitosubashi on Knowledge Management" Singapore, John Wiley & Sons (Asia) Ptw.Ltd.2004:67

tacit knowledge, through the minds of other individuals like groups or teams. In this phase, the external interaction process begins (in a way which means outside the individual's mind) between the individual and others, whether they are work colleagues, suppliers or beneficiaries of the work and services of the organization. The motivator element to this interaction will be participating in experiments and work practices. Through discussion, dialogue, sharing ideas, and brainstorming with the minds of others, the tacit knowledge crystallizes into a new form.

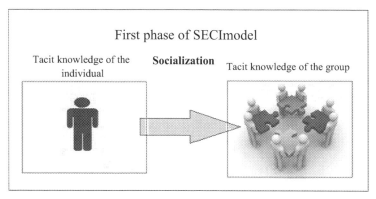

Figure 20: Socialization – the first
phase of the SECI model

If we are to look at this knowledge before and after the socialization step, it would be portrayed as follows:

Tacit knowledge (individual) in first figure before interaction with the others

New tacit

(collective) knowledge

This is the area where the individual moves alone. This is its space and its own world

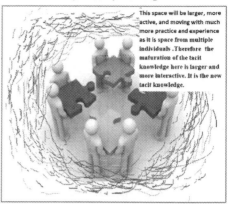

This space will be larger, more active, and moving with much more practice and experience as it is space from multiple individuals .Therefore the maturation of the tacit knowledge here is larger and more interactive. It is the new tacit knowledge.

Figure 21: Tacit knowledge before and after specialization.
The colored lines represent tacit knowledge.

Second phase - externalization: externalization and expressing

In this phase, we need to embody the knowledge that we acquired in the first phase and apply it in the form of laws, new methods of work, novel ideas, new products, or new procedures. In this phase knowledge enters another form, unlike the tacit that was hidden in the minds. It is explicit knowledge or external in the form of symbols, numbers, models or description.

Third Phase - combination: construction, collection, and integration

Through movement of the now explicit knowledge, additions and modifications begin to be made by others. Explicit knowledge is transmitted from its first, more simplistic form to a more complicated form that occurs as a result of the continuous interaction process, in which our knowledge develops through applications and observations.

For example, the **smart reader** system in a smart phones application (that does not exceed $99) reads all the contents of a smart phone out, so as to enable a blind person to use the different functions in a smart phone. This idea, when first used, was applied on a device the size of an electrical washer and it had a price tag of fifty thousand dollars. This portrays how our knowledge becomes developed and reaches a more advanced form, that was easier, smaller in cost, and more advantageous to a larger number of people.

Fourth phase – internalization

In this phase, the produced explicit knowledge goes back to its original form, reduced back through the whole organization to tacit knowledge, added to the minds of individuals and becoming a component that didn't exist in that form before. It makes each individual's cognitive components grow and become stronger, which prepares it for a new cognitive start that would generate new products, new outcomes, and new forms, thus continuously moving in a spiral process.

To summarize the SECI Model:

- The first origin of knowledge, particularly tacit knowledge, is what we have in our minds.
- Following that, the realized knowledge needs a holder rich with mental and cognitive motivations, as well as the existence of another that is ready to listen and accept the ideas, especially new ideas, in a way that would lead to the achievement of psychological gratification to knowledge owners.
- The creation of a positive climate is critical to accept a new idea and accordingly, spreading it at the level of the organization.
- The spiral movement for knowledge needs an optimum environment to germinate and plant the flowers of knowledge, in order to grow and succeed in the organization. Nonaka called such an environment knowledge space or knowledge place.[39]

---

[39] Nonaka, I. (1994). "A Dynamic Theory of Organizational Knowledge Creation", *Organization Science*, 5 (1). 14-37.

CHAPTER VIII

In this Chapter:

- Modern Cognitive Theory on Integrated Cognitive Structure, Stem Cells Cognitive Theory (SCC)
- Stem cells cognitive as a meaning and a concept
- Stem cells and cognitive stem cell properties
- Cognitive walls: filtering of cognitive components.

The Modern Cognitive Theory in the Integrated Cognitive Construction – Stem Cells Cognitive Theory (SCC)

Many literatures on the matter of knowledge begin with going through the meaning of knowledge quickly, curtly, and abstrusely, that often all you get out of it is confusion. Some of them go through the meaning of knowledge in the language dictionaries and others start with the creation of the universe. They then ask their question: Is knowledge old or modern? Thus, our journey to knowledge passes without understanding knowledge or it's dynamics.

My motive since I started my journey with this book is to discover knowledge, to elucidate it as a story and a reality that we all live in and to understand its mobility. How does it work? How does it compose? How it moves inside us? How to compose it and how to preserve?

I have divided my literature into several parts. The goal of the first part was to explain the creative and innovative nature of knowledge and what we know about its development as a science. Next, I will address its management. How to manage it? How to motivate its movement within our organizations? How to make it a fact instead of just words and figures?

My concern is to build knowledge, depending on practical experiences from the problems of organizations, companies, and individuals in all sectors and domains around the world along with my experience with knowledge in training, education, guidance, and counseling for more than twenty-five years. This theory was not established out of thin air, or through rigid or theoretical research that is far from the field of employment and the problems of organizations and individuals in different societies, environments, cultures, and civilizations.

The modern theory in integrated cognitive construction that I have named the Stem Cells Cognitive Theory (SCC) was concluded from real life experiences and examples.

Cognitive stem cells between meaning and concept

So, why Cognitive stem cells? How does it relate to knowledge and the expression of cognitive construction in a true and integrated quality?

Science has not discovered yet what knowledge does with the mind and its cells. What does knowledge do with the strength of cells and their renewal and maintenance? What does knowledge do to open doors, possibilities, and capabilities like no other thing can?

First, we must ask, what are stem cells?

The human body is composed of two hundred and forty species of cells, all of which rise from stem cells. These are cells which are formed during the first days of embryonic fertilization and appears after the fertilization of an egg. At this stage, specifically, there are no limits for the possibilities of stem cells. It lays the beginning of the establishment phase for all types of cells (brain, heart, skin, lungs, pancreas, liver, eye, and all other organs).

Stem cells and cognitive stem cell properties

Stem Cells have two utmost characteristics:

The first characteristic is the ability to divide and the ability for constant renewal, just like knowledge. Through the movement of the mind with its components and cognitive precipitations, as explained previously in many realistic examples and stories starting from Michael to David Frost, you can see thousands of cognitive outputs and what cognitive creativity can generate.

The second characteristic is its ability to be unique. That is to say, it can become of any type of cell; whether they are heart cells, pancreas cells, liver cells or any other type of cell that the body needs in its composition. It is the same situation with knowledge. Wherever you direct knowledge and direct your mind, with your concentration and imagination focused towards it, you will generate endless kinds, types, forms and species of knowledge. Examples of this knowledge is physical knowledge, technological knowledge, mathematical knowledge, administrative knowledge, geological knowledge, medical knowledge, astronomical knowledge, musical knowledge, literary knowledge, and so on.

Science will prove that knowledge has many effects on the health of the mind and memory. It will prove that many cells die and cannot be renewed, because its renewal is subjected to your movement, vigilance, strengthening, endowments and memory (plasticity). Stem cells have proven that they will be the future of modern medicine. It is believed that within a few years medicine will not need for drugs, and that therapy will be directly by stem cells.[40]

Stem cells' name is derived from the word (stem), because the human body is like a tree with roots, its stem is the base that holds and connects

---

[40] http://www.chla.org/site/c.ipINKTOAJsG/b.8289595/k.525F/Ahmed_ElHashash_PhD_Lab.htm#.VOlJlvmUcrI

it together and knowledge is the fruit you reap from this tree. Knowledge is the basis for building the mind and strengthening, regeneration, maintenance, reproduction, activeness, attention, and wakefulness of its cells.

Cognitive walls: filtering of cognitive components

Now, we are faced with two types of what can be designated as cognitive components:

The first type: This is what comes to us through the five senses; it starts since the early stages of our lives.

The second type: This is what we get through the educational process with its various stages, through understanding or memorization and any means of reading or training for a career, a job, a practice, or an experience.

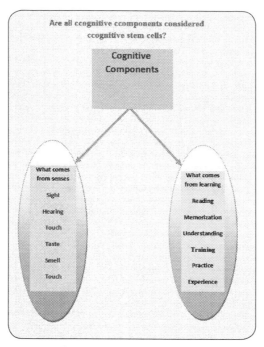

Figure 22: What constitutes a cognitive component

To have something be, not just a cognitive component, but a stem cells cognitive component it must follow the rules of cognitive construction, the first two having already been mentioned in the previous chapters.

The third rule in cognitive construction

All that we cannot remember is not considered a cognitive component; it is unknown, and so you become equal to one who is ignorant of it. All that is lost from your memory, or what you do not understand the meaning of or reference to, is meaningless to you. Hence, no desired knowledge will be built on that which is non-existent or unknown.

To illustrate this rule, let's look at the following examples.

The first example

If someone was to learn that a red traffic signal is for stopping, then an incident happened to them and they lost a part of their memory. If they can no longer remember the meaning of the red traffic signal, would they will stop? Of course not; it would represent nothing in their current memory.

The second example[41]

Terry Jones is fifty years old. When he awoke as usual, he went to take a shower then eat his breakfast. Suddenly, something happened while he was in the shower that made him almost lose his mind. He stretched out his hand to take the shampoo, and found that there is more than one kind, so he tried to read what was written on the shampoo, to make sure that it is the kind that he prefers. But he could not read any more than the letters B, C, V ...., he did not understand any of it. He took the other one, and read the same letters, but they did not mean a thing to his memory. He decided to have breakfast then because he reasoned that it maybe was hunger that caused this. He requested the breakfast menu at the restaurant and tried to read, but again he did not see anything other than the letters A, K, B, C, D. He did not understand them and left the restaurant in a daze. So, he immediately went to see a specialist. His story amazed the neuroscientists at the University of London. They found that he had a damaged area in his brain, so, instead of being able normally, he was reading the words like a child did. He saw the letters, but the part of his brain responsible for recalling the image significance (visual information) had been destroyed. Neuroscientists did not know the secret behind what happened?

In both the above examples, individuals were not able to use or build their actions on knowledge they had, because it was either inaccessible to them or it was something that they can no longer apprehend.

---

[41] The journalist "Rita Carter", in cooperation with (BBC). https://vimeo.com/38442002 BBC documentary why reading matters on Vimeo

So, how can you compose knowledge for something that does not exist. If you recall the story of Michael and how he reached his decision, you will now realize that it was because he comprehended that there is a difference between what he saw in that fire, and all the incidents he saw during twenty-year of experience. What Michael had is both a **cognitive component and a stem cells component (SCC)**, because when his mind recollected the previous images of all he has seen, he found in this knowledge an explanation to what he was seeing. Once again, I must reiterate: cognitive matter is not a matter of components, information, data, etc., but the secret lies in the way you choose to deal with the components that you receive. Now we can also clearly say, that in the carpenters' story mentioned earlier, what the first carpenter had, was maybe a cognitive component because he had the knowledge. On the other hand, the second carpenter had both the cognitive components and the stem cells cognitive components, which produced and resulted in a new knowledge.

It will not be an exaggeration if I say that everything that enters your mind has a degree of frequency and vibration that constitutes the shape of cognitive component you have and leaves its imprint. The power or weakness of the frequency is what constitutes the input or cognitive component you have. The ability to recollect the cognitive components is not sufficient. These components need to have the capacity to produce new knowledge.

The evidence for this comes from the fact that anyone who has information or data and has the capacity to recollect it from memory, cannot automatically produce new knowledge or be innovative. They can know how to perform, constitute, make something or how to conduct or manage something or skill. But all that, solely, does not cause creativity.

> ## The fourth rule in cognitive construction
>
> The quantity and quality of cognitive components,
> whatever its types or sources, does not guarantee
> production or output of new knowledge.

The degree of an individual's inclination, desire, yearning, querying, and continuity of research are elements that constitute the energy, frequency, strength, and weakness of knowledge. Also, they are what triggers the birth of new knowledge and the formation of the cognitive fetus. One factor cannot constitute new knowledge in isolation from other factors; they are a communicated ring that strengthens and nourishes each other.

To illustrate this with an example,
Mark and Jim are friends who like to work out together. For a month, they continued together in their hard exercises and achieved good initial results. Suddenly, and without any obvious reason, Mark stopped attending the training. Jim, on the other hand, continued on with his training and followed up on everything related to the sport of bodybuilding that he could find. He attended matches, participated in some, and watched videos of previous matches. He read books and references and learned from them how to better his workout regimen. He asked experts, followed world champions and their stories, to know how they reached what they have achieved of precedence globally or internationally. At every moment, he visualized himself as a world champion in bodybuilding. He continued, and with every success his determination grew. After seven years of continuous and consecutive work, he finally achieved **his dream and won the world championship in body building.**

The period which Mark worked out in did not exceed a month. Are the cognitive components of bodybuilding between Mark and Jim equal?

Can you make Mark, who left the sport of bodybuilding for a long time and whose body probably returned to what it was or even worse, take part in a match against Jim? As it is with sports like bodybuilding, it is also true with knowledge. In sports, you cannot succeed without energy, effort, perseverance, patience, continuity, and sustainability. The same is true with knowledge. You need all these factors for successful knowledge training.

It the same with cognitive components and SCC; they need to be in a continuous and ongoing motion and activity until you become accustomed to them and they become second nature. Knowledge is not reading for an hour, doing exercises for two hours, or training for a week. Anything new you do when your mind is distracted cannot be a cognitive component nor knowledge for stem cells. You need to be fully prepared to gain these new cognitive components and use them. So how do we know if we have enough desire, inclination etc. to make the cut?

First: If the degree of inclination, desire and other factors is non-existent, there will not be a cognitive component nor SCC.

This is what happens when an individual has the information or data but does not have the desire or inclination to make anything of it. He hopes the work hours ends soon to forget about it. This will never yield cognitive components nor SCC. This is incidentally, also the fifth rule in counting something as a cognitive component.

> The fifth rule in cognitive construction
>
> If the degree of desire and inclination towards what you want to do, is nonexistent, there will be no value to the components.

Second: If the degree of inclination, desire and other factors is weak, we will have cognitive component with a weak frequency power that does not prevent anything nor perform anything. It cannot be SCC; weak and inactive movement which is closer to nonexistence, will not be utilized. If an individual remained at this level, he will not be eligible to produce new knowledge.

Third: If the degree of inclination, desire and other factors is active, we can consider it as a cognitive component. In this case the individual would be qualified to form SCC, provided that, the individual tries hard to raise his abilities, energies, determination, desire, inclination, and motivation to reach an even higher degree of activity.

Fourth: If the degree of inclination, desire and other factors is highly active, we can say that the individuals' components are cognitive component and SCC. It is possible that he could reach a higher degree of new knowledge and creativity.

Fifth: If the degree of inclination, desire and other factors is super-active, the individual will be qualified to form and produce components of cognitive and super active SCC. The achievement of creativity is easy, provided that maintenance and continuity does not stop.

There is variation in strength and capacity of talents and capabilities between people. We are different in our talents, capabilities, and energies. Someone may have a high degree of imagination whereas another might have a high talent in memorization while another may have the ability to debate and find connections between different topics easily, while another might take much longer to reach the same conclusions. Darwin used to say that he is not quick-witted, but he has the patience needed for observation. Many others might not have this talent. He was excellent in the accurate observation of things and noticing what others fail to, but he did not have the talent of memorizing, and absolutely hated it.

Niels Bohr, the famous scientist who founded the quantum mechanics theory, was a slow thinker. He would take time to absorb information, whereas Einstein was excellent in imagination. Even among these great scientists, no two were the same.

So, if we are to look back at all these rules mentioned, it can be depicted collectively in the following table:

	First Wall	Second Wall			Third Wall	
Cognitive Components	Not a Cognitive Component nor a Stem Cells Cognitive (SCC)				Talents and Capabilities	
		Existence kind	Existence degree	Component and Cells		
What enters through the five senses and what enters through learning	Cannot be recollected	Inclination	Non-existence	Not a Cognitive Component nor a Stem Cells Cognitive (SCC)	The more active talents and capacities, the highest access and influence to knowledge	Knowledge
		Desire				
		Eagerness	Weak	Weak Cognitive Component and not Stem Cells Cognitive (SCC)		
		Worry				
Reading		Pursuance				
		Search	Active	Cognitive Component qualified to be Stem Cells Cognitive (SCC)		
Memorization		Continuity				
Understanding			High-Activity	A Cognitive Component and a Stem Cells Cognitive (SCC)		
Training						
Practice			Hyper-Activity	A Cognitive Component and a Stem Cells Cognitive with high activity		
Experience						

Table 1: What constitutes a cognitive component and a stem cells cognitive

I will conclude this part with Dr. Michio Kaku, the American Japanese scientist, one of the pioneering physicists at New York University, who said in his speech about cognitive curiosity in education that he thinks the educational process crushes cognitive curiosity. This is the result of forcing students to memorize large amounts of facts and numbers., which stems from the idea that science is memorization, which is a fatal error.

On one occasion his daughter had an exam, where she had to memorize a set of facts and numbers about metals and other facts for a Geology exam. Upon briefing the manual, he did not see anything related to the real motivation of geological research and the movement of continental budge, which is the main principle behind the science of Geology. However, the exam required her to memorize a tremendous amount of minerals and other things, which caused her to say she never wants to be a scientist! His frustration at that point knew no bounds. This education and specifically this exam was crushing his daughters' cognitive curiosity. It was a grave disservice to the whole generation. [42]

---

[42] Dr. Michio Kaku: The Problem with the learning system in school https://vimeo. com/30066733 Video for Dr. Michio Kaku: The Problem with the learning system in school - Oct 5, 2011- "by C Harper

CHAPTER IX

In his chapter we will discuss:

- Desire scales
- Knowledge spiral in accordance with the stem cell cognitive theory (SCC)
- Socialization secrets
- The secret that exhausted Darwin

Desire scales

These are the scales suggested to measure the desire of an individual.

1 - Observation

Accurate observation is based on understanding and analysis. It is required to help identify the individual desires and trend. Once you identify your desires you can move towards fulfilling them. Careful observation connects you to the real potential and orientations of an individual.

In illustrate this point let's consider the following example.
While in college, Darwin would attend the lectures of Professor John Stevens Henslow. He liked the different subjects Henslow talked about and the relation between them grew closer. Henslow would often invite him over for dinners where they would discuss different topics they had common interests in. Henslow was well-versed at entomology, plant science, marine biology, the science of metal work, chemistry, and geology. He became aware that Darwin was not a normal student, and had in fact unusual potentials and capabilities so he started treating him as a mentor. Darwin would accompany him everywhere, trying to learn as much as he could from him.

One day, Darwin went back home to find that he had received a message from Professor Henslow, telling him about a voyage about to commence by the British exploration vessel – the Beagles. The captain of this ship, based on the recommendation of Henslow, was allowing Darwin to accompany them on this exploratory trip around the world, on a voluntary basis without pay. But, this would mean that he had to leave school for a while. When he brought this matter to the attention of his father, he flatly refused until Henslow reassured him that Darwin had extraordinary abilities and he expected a bright future for him.

If Henslow had not observed Darwin closely and concluded that his abilities would be of great benefit for science, and if had not nominated him for that scientific journey that changed his life, Darwin would not have become a scientist.

2 - Permanent active participation.

An individual has to be continuously actively participating in work groups or scientific and professional associations (like workshops or laboratories), supervised by scientists with the ability, the know-how, the experience and the wisdom to analyze and identify the potential of individuals and motivate and develop it. This participation whether scientific, intellectual, literary or professional, is considered as a means of measuring the orientation towards a certain type of science, art or literature.

3 - Research and worksheets.

For this to succeed, training must start at an early stage to teach an individual how to take part in correct scientific research practices and how to rely on the correct sources.

4 - Cognitive identity card.

The cognitive identity card is a cognitive condition record that includes a register covering the individual's history since early childhood in terms of hobbies, inclinations, abilities, orientations, extent of proficiency, and potential. Based on this record the individual is directed to appropriate educational specialties, associations, and scientific, literary and artistic clubs so that a follow up by specialists can be conducted on the individual at every age group. If we help our children grow according to the guidance, motivation and stimulation of early scientific knowledge-based structure, we will have adults with creative capabilities to build a strong nation based on knowledge.

When we talk about the cognitive identity card, we mean the accurate and scientific follow-up of an individual's desire and abilities since the early stages of their life, and the measures conducted to develop this individual in a manner that guarantees reinforcing him/her in whatever field they desire.

Now in terms of SCC, does the producer of knowledge truly have cognitive knowledge?

The producer of knowledge would have the true form of knowledge because they produced it, relying on his/her kinetic and mental energy, cognitive container, and cognitive stem cells. Examples of knowledge producers are Einstein's theory and Newton's Law. This knowledge goes back to its owner since the innovator is always connected to their cognitive outputs as soon as it is produced or generated.

What about the hierarchy of knowledge, from the perspective of the Stem Cells Cognitive (SCC) theory?

Knowledge shouldn't be placed in a frame or dealt with as an equation. It has overlapping structure and is not formed in this way. The idea of the hierarchy of knowledge would not produce any benefits in the area of integrated cognitive restructuring. It is advisable that the idea of the hierarchy of knowledge is left aside because knowledge cannot be structured in this way.

The knowledge spiral in light of the Stem Cells Cognitive theory (SCC)

Before discussing the knowledge spiral, we should first deal with the following questions:

- Why do we insist on talking about the knowledge spiral? And what is the secret behind it?
- What is the importance of collective participation in the process of cognitive restructuring?
- Is cognitive restructuring based on collective participation and if so, can we only produce knowledge through this collective form?

It is very important to answer the above questions in order to understand cognitive restructuring. It is important as well to understand the secrets behind cognitive restructuring, since knowledge is not forms and models to be made without understanding its secrets and the reasons for its existence and structure. This can help in understanding the two most important matters in cognitive restructuring. First, it will explain what it is that we are trying to restructure. Second, it will help in understanding the components of the cognitive restructuring so as to serve the process of creation, innovation, and the development of talents, opening the door for inspiration and stimulating the thinking process.

The knowledge spiral, according to Nonaka and Takeuchi, starts as tacit knowledge, produced by an individual and circulated among the members of a group who in turn develop the same knowledge so that it becomes a collective tacit knowledge which spreads beyond the group and becomes apparent knowledge.

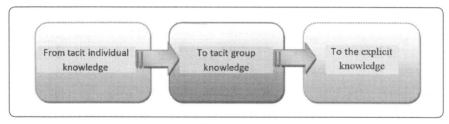

Figure 23: Evolution of knowledge from tacit to explicit.

So, why do we insist on talking about the knowledge spiral? And what is the secret behind it?

Spiral or helical movement means a sequential rotational movement of the body around its axis. Knowledge moves up in the context of its composition in a sequential and spiral manner around its axis and develops continually in this way? This development of knowledge happens in the mind of the individual. When the cognition and cognitive stem cells are of super active movement they continuously move, even while we are asleep or busy. This happens when the matter occupies much space in our mind. Experiments have proven that the human mind never stops working even while we are asleep, as it processes what we think deeply about. This is what we mean by the secret of knowledge in reviving, renewing, and maintaining nerve cells. Without this, nerve cells are subjected to atrophy or death. With the lapse of time and with the weakness and atrophy of the nerve cells, weakness of memory, and decline of mental and cognitive capabilities pass from generation to generation until a time comes when the ratio of dementia, Alzheimer or memory loss rises. Scientific studies report a rise in the ratio of dementia all over the world. What is even more dangerous, is that young people suffer from dementia at younger ages than ever seen before.

When we think of a new idea, a subject of science, a solution to a problem or the reasons for a phenomenon, all of this represents brainstorming. Hundreds or thousands of messages move between synapses which are in turn strengthened with the electric movement or chemical messages. This, subsequently, opens the door to capabilities and talents which we might not have known existed before.

Proof of this are the studies made on Einstein's brain after his death. It was found that the number of glial cells in his brain exceeds the average number in the normal human being by 15%. Other studies conducted on taxi drivers in Britain, have shown that the hippocampus, which is the part located above the ear on both sides of the brain and used to deduce or recall locations, was larger than others. Einstein might or might not have started out with larger number of glial cells, and the taxi drivers could have had a normal size hippocampus when they first started or not. The point is that if Einstein had not used his intellect to continuously ask questions and solve problems, and if these taxi drivers had changed professions or decided to use a GPS instead of depending on their memories, the end result would have been atrophy. The act of continuous use of their faculties and growing their capabilities and intellects is what kept those brain regions alive and active. Hence knowledge spiral is an expression of cognition within the mind since the beginning of the first stages of the formation, enrichment, and embryonic construction. It grows day after day. The contact between the individual and the group develops the knowledge produced by the individual to new knowledge.

This is the secret of knowledge spiral and why we accept it as a means of cognitive restructuring.

Socialization secrets

Why is socialization important in cognitive restructuring?

The same question can be asked in another way: Why do birds, animals, and fish migrate for thousands of miles together? Why do birds not travel individually? **What is the secret behind collective work?** Is collective work essential for cognitive restructuring? If cognitive restructuring is an individual process, then why do they prefer working collectively?

A short time ago, scientists revealed some of the answers to these questions as they were trying to determine why birds fly in a V shaped formation. They discovered that this manner of flight eases the energy burden on the entire group.

The secret that exhausted Darwin

This phenomenon may intersect with the secret that bewildered Darwin, who spent much effort and time to find an answer to these questions: What is the reason for diversification of living organisms? Why are there long beaked birds, birds with wide beaks, flat beaks, and birds with pointed beaks? Why do some birds with wings fly while others don't? What is the secret behind this?

As a result of these questions, he developed the theory of evolution and natural selection. But I think it goes on much deeper than that. The secret lies in the diversity of energy.

Everything in the universe has energy, frequency, and wavelength. Why are some people surprised about this if the whole universe began with a tremendous energy which is the basic component of everything?

Energy is constant in the entire universe since it began. It does not change, and everything in the universe is formed based on this frequency. The musical scale is not played without the multiplicity of grades and frequencies, and our ears would not acclaim or accept it, without them. The entire universe is based on pluralism. Science will realize that diversity, plurality, and frequency are the universe's balance. Each frequency and shape represents part of the tune and the balanced language of the universe.

It has been proved that the survival of the universe is based on biodiversity. The ruin of biodiversity means the collapse and end of the whole universe. If energy loses its balance, the whole universe will come to an end. Energy balance is the secret of its diversity, and its diversity is the secret of the survival of the universe.

This secret was realized by Ernst Mayr, a professor of Biology at Harvard University and one of the founders of the Neo-Darwinism who occupies the chair of Alexander Aksai. He is a pioneer in ornithology, taxonomy, and the history and philosophy of biology, who has achieved the highest degree in evolutionary biology and in the history of science.

Meyer after solving this mystery stated that, the larger the size of a species, the slower is its development, since it has become idle in terms of evolution.

As true as this is, it would also mean that the universe had excluded species from evolution based on their size, which would have inevitably lead to the extinction of these species and the end of life since the world cannot place restrictions on size, and only survive on species that are within a specific size limit. Thus, diversity and antithesis, compulsion and heterogeneous oscillation are all important for the life cycle.

Feeling hungry is an innate feeling without which the living organism does not move to feed itself. Fear is an innate feeling without which species cannot keep their lives and maintain their survival. Unless the living organism satisfies its sexual desire, its survival is not maintained. And so, such innate feelings exist to maintain survival of life. These are mechanisms for the universe to continue. In this way, the universe and the other creatures remain, and any failure or incompliance results in a threat for survival.

Darwin believed in the brutality of nature, when he saw strong animals mercilessly killing weaker animals. He thought deeply on this matter due to his sensitive nature. He saw an insect killing another weaker insect mercilessly, and therefore, he believed in the idea of the survival of the fittest, on which many scientific laws have been based. The fact is, the law of the whole universe is based on diversity, but not only biodiversity. It is diversity in everything, so as to complete the power circle and to insure the survival of the universe.

> ### The sixth rule in cognitive construction
>
> When an individual exercises a super active cognitive restructuring the nerve connectors and cells become in constant activity and maintenance. This guarantees survival. It opens the door before talents and strengthens and supports them. This is a protection for the human mind from all known and potential diseases. The absence of active cognitive restructuring will result in threats for the humankind. This means that Alzheimer's is not the only danger in absence of active cognitive restructuring. Thus, man's survival requires not only knowledge but also knowledge diversity.

Some people may note that they have enjoyed a healthy life without knowledge, so what is the reason to fear?

To answer this question, let's look at the Ayis Mellifera, the most important honey producing bee in the world. Beekeeping flourished around 4000 BC, and people lived on its several benefits for a long time. On the Korean Peninsula, the local Asian bees and a kind of mites co-existed. The bees evolved their capabilities and defenses to be accustomed to living with the mites without suffering any injury, and so they lived safely for ages. Then, there was a transfer of large number of European honey bees (the Ayis Mellifera) from Europe to the Korean Peninsula through Siberia, and all of a sudden, the bees began leaving their nests and a large number of bees died. The breeders and dealers were in a state of terror, they had lost their source of income.

Dr. Dennis Anderson, the famous Australian scientist came to discover that there is a species of mite, which have co-existed with Asian honey bees on the Korean peninsula for millions of years, that had a genetic mutation and the European bees could not cope with them. These mites could devastate the defensive abilities of the bees. They were called the Varroa destructor mite, or the vampire mite. Sixty-five years later, the Varroa destructor mite spread has started threatening the existence of honey bees all over the world.

Researchers used toxic pesticides, but with time the mites became resistant to them. Scientists now have to develop their pesticides every year, otherwise the mites will acquire immunity and develop their abilities and defenses.

The same thing that happened with the European bees could happen to us. When we grow a lazy, laid back attitude instead of constantly growing and evolving, there is no guarantee that we wouldn't face something in our lives that would challenge and break us. The Varroa destructor mite faced the challenge of a new bee by evolving and destroying them. Diversity and permanent change is the secret of the survival of the universe. Force and counterforce in a harmonious movement result in energies integrities. Here exists the secret of total energy, which surpasses the individual energy. The diversity of energies fulfills energies complementarity and balance. Individual energy cannot achieve the efforts achieved by total energy. Likewise, a group protection will always be stronger than an individual protection. The will of a group is, of course, stronger than the will of an individual.

Diversity and antagonism is not at all surprising. It is the secret of life and the key for survival. This shouldn't be interpreted as struggle for existence, the brutality of nature, or natural selection. This is just the surface of the equation; however, its content, structure and secret are much greater and deeper.

In stringed instruments, an individual string cannot delight you. A group of strings in the instrument work together to make you enjoy listening to a beautiful melody.

Figure 24: A French horn

If you think about the melody emitted by a trumpet or horn, like the French horn **(figure 25)**, you will find that it is formed by controlling the movement of air and vibrations, issued by the musician's mouth or by pressing keys, and with every keystroke you hear a different sound that completes the melody. The alteration of sounds and tones here came as a result of change in vibrations. When the vibrations made by a musical instrument meets with the vibrations inside you on the same wave you feel happy. If the external vibrations do not meet the internal vibrations you feel something strange or uncomfortable; so, whales become disturbed and lose their appetite for food and even move away at full speed when they feel noise that disturbs them.

Bats know the secret of the impact of frequency on enemy bats who desire to steal their food, so they cause their enemy bats to become mentally disoriented. When bats feel that that their enemy is close they disturb their enemy by releasing high frequency waves. When bats launch raids on their prey in the dark they release high frequency sound waves. This process is termed as reverberation.

The whales, as well, have realized the secret of frequencies.[43] They use vibrations to entrap their preys. Whales, in addition have a strong memory, that enables them to remember the sounds of other whales that have come near them in the past twenty years.

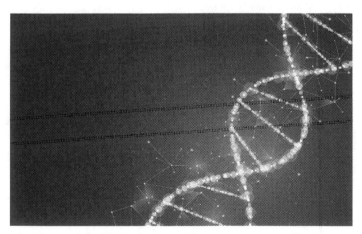

Figure 25: DNA that encodes our genetic make-up

---

[43] http://www.bbc.com/news/magazine-

Sound vibrations can even affect DNA to a great extent[44], [45], and the secret of life is concealed therein for hundreds and thousands of years after death.

How cruel nature is, where the strong animal feeds on the weaker one. Life, in this way, is based on the struggle for survival, and the weak have no place, so survival is for the strongest or the fittest. This is the base for Darwin's Law of Evolution by natural selection.

It is my opinion that there isn't any random natural selection.
The reason for this is the integrated reactive balanced power (the balance of the universe's energy). This is required for the survival and maintenance of the universe. Life is based on an integrated law. You may imagine it as a struggle. This is not true. It is a matter of energy transfer from one form to another, so that the universe remains balanced and renewed in a continuous non-stop movement.

Now, it has been made clear that total energy is required for knowledge.
Knowledge cannot be formed without this energy. However, bear in mind that there is a difference between cognitive restructuring and cognitive formation. Knowledge is made individually in terms of origin and formation. The same applies to the field of research. The role of the researcher as regards to the research outcome is the same as the role of the incubator to the newly born baby whose development has not been completed. The role of the group here in the research process is to maintain the newly produced knowledge. However, it is wrong to believe that knowledge in this way is built by the group. Cognitive restructuring is originally individual. The individual is its builder and modeler. The group function is to maintain the newly born knowledge. To sum up, cognitive restructuring is based on individual

---

[44] http://www.wakingtimes.com/2014/12/26/human-dna-reprogrammable-light-sound-frequency-vibration/

[45] http://undergroundhealthreporter.com/dna-science-and-reprograming-your-dna/#axzz3jZ0whmcI

effort. The role of the group is essential. In the complementary cognitive restructuring the individual has a role and the group has another role.

....

The seventh rule in knowledge construction

The role of the group in the balanced complementary cognitive structure in institutions, companies, and research centers is basic. The role of the group is required to maintain the produced knowledge. It is the energy carrier that helps the individual who is the originator of that knowledge. Without the group, knowledge cannot be complete.

If you want to understand the universe, think of energy, frequency and vibration.
Nikola Tesla [46]
(1856-1943 AD)

_____

[46] **Nikola Tesla:** Nikola Tesla is in the list of the greatest scientists and inventors of all time. He was born in Croatia in the era of the Austrian Empire, later became a US citizen, was known for his contributions in the field of high electromagnetic energy in the late nineteenth century. He was dubbed the father of physics and the inventor of the twentieth century. Among his most famous inventions are the AC, radio, remote control devices, lasers, telecommunications, and light control and distribution.

CHAPTER X

In this chapter, we will discuss:

- The thoughts affecting the building of spiral and SECI model
- A mind's story
- The SECI Model of Stem Cells Cognitive (SCC)
- The reality of the individuality and collectivity in the cognitive structure process
- Cognitive formation dimensions as per stem cells cognitive
- Types of the cognitive stem cells

The thoughts affecting the building of spiral and SECI model

The collective Japanese mode of thinking, which is rooted in the Japanese culture, has a clear impact on the concept of the spiral, as well as the SECI model. All matters discussed by Nonaka and Takashi, who were born in Japan, over the cognitive structure, reflected the depth of the Japanese civilization, especially with regard to teamwork. No nation has a strong build for team work and the spirit of team as the Japanese nation. They do not know the abstract individual thinking or the abstract individual creativity (Ego), as defined by western civilizations, countries, peoples, and attitudes. Therefore, it is no secret that the Japanese application of knowledge and the cognitive structure is completely different from the western application of the cognitive structure. Hence, you can see the impact of the environment, culture, and civilization on the cognitive structure; therefore, we could say that:

It is not recommended to use a particular model of cognitive structure and application, without taking into account matters that fit the environment and culture prevailing among the members of this environment.

The eight rule in knowledge construction

The accelerated and hasty use of a cognitive structure without prior appropriate preparation is affecting the validity and straightness of the structure and causing it to fail in achieving the desired results. Experienced scientists should take into account conditions of the dominant culture and matters suitable for such environments, in which this structure will be applied, through an accurate, careful, and wise study. Such scientists should experience the conditions, culture, and circumstances of such environments; otherwise, we will fail to know the nature of our structure and its surroundings and circumstances of success. No specific models are recommended, even if they succeed in a particular environment and a particular culture with potentials and capabilities differing from this environment, culture and potentials.

The main reason for the partial success achieved by the application of the spiral model in some western environments, even with a lack of the collectivism attitude that the Japanese society is well-known for, is not attributed to the individualism of the Western culture but instead to simply urgent need. Let us look into this in some detail.

A Mind's Story

Figure 26: Hand crafted shoes

There was a time in the past, where things like shoes were made by hand. The shoemaker would inspect the quality of the leather after taking it from a merchant specialized in selling leather. He would then go to his shop and start making a masterpiece, where every detail is of utmost importance and made with absolute care.

Figure 27: Sowing the bottom of the shoe

He would bring out the wood block, which he created and designed by his own hands. On the desk used for extending the leather, the shoemaker would choose the type he wants for designing the shoes as per the size of the person who wants the shoes. Afterwards, he would bring a knife to cut off the leather. Then, he would put this internal cover made of carton and spray the wood block with a type of powder, so that the leather would not stick to the block and make it easy to take out after completing the shoes. Then, he would use the nails he bought and begin fixing the nails in the leather after cutting and designing the leather to the block. Next, he would put the cover on the heel and start cutting the extra parts by the knife after softening them using sandpaper. Following that, he would knock them by his hands to test them. Subsequently, the shoemaker would use the thread and needle to sew the bottom of the shoe with the upper part. Then, he softens it with sandpaper or a piece of glass. Finally, he paints the heels in the same color of the leather to give it a dark color.

In the end, the shoemaker manufactures the best, strongest, and most beautiful hand-made shoes which are now lamented as masterpieces and sold for many times the price of regular shoes.

This is an example of how industries, in their origin, were of high quality and elegance. Do you imagine that such a shoe would have a broken heel after the first wear? Recently, what is becoming more and more common is that manufacturers withdraw from the market millions of cars, because the brakes have a fault that could cause accidents and deaths. These industries have killed most of the collective innovative and integrated spirit, whose innovations cannot be compensated, especially through the use of modern technological machines. Such industries cannot make up for the creations of the collective mind and what the mind can make for man, his abilities, vitality, activity, resistance, defenses, and the minds' strong, communicative and movement cells (Cognitive Neural Chemical Electromagnetic).

Figure 28: The present state of shoe making

So, are workers, professors, physicians, and artists today the same as they were in the past? Everyone knows the answer to this question, at least subconsciously. The better question to ask is this:

Have the cognitive and collective minds crumbled?

Imagine that the same shoemaker we followed above is now working in a shoe factory, that is operated by the latest technological devices, for a period of fifteen years. This worker was given the duty to specialize in heels, but only heels. He is to have nothing to do with the rest of the shoe. What would the result be?

Over a period of fifteen years, this great encyclopedic, cognitive and collective mind, who was fascinated with every part of the shoe, has become limited only to the heels. Modern industries took the worker away from the world of leather and the world of design, and stuck him in the monotony of focusing on one part of the shoe. What a loss! All his skills and his abilities confined and not allowed to be creative. **This is fragmentation of the cognitive mind.**

Now, let us look at the following three images together and see what we can conclude from them:

Figure 29: The art of leather making

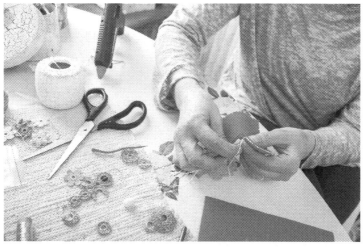

Figure 30: The art of crafting

Figure 31: The art of wood work

What is the dire need for creativity in the 3 pictures above? And what is the link between creativity and teamwork, which is necessary to achieve creativity and develop new knowledge?

Creativity has become an urgent issue especially in industries that are trying to stay on the top of the global market. It has become a necessary factor for organizations to maintain their presence and to compete with each other, in addition to coping with the rapidly growing technological advances.

As we said before, mere creativity and knowledge-based super creativity is not enough. It is necessary to adopt the principle of teamwork to achieve this creativity, which most of our businesses lack today. Thus, the spirit of work as one team or an integrated group has returned to the western civilization after it was confined to a particular culture and a particular civilization. We gave an example of the Japanese environment and how the combination of creativity and team work led to exemplar results in their industries. For this reason, teamwork and creativity have become an urgent need.

International companies have done their utmost to promote creativity by offering shares worth millions, not just thousands of dollars, in their businesses to creative and specialized individuals. They do so with the aim of extracting new knowledge and creativity in any form. Many of the well-known international companies, such as Microsoft, Apple, and Google have followed this trend and it is one of the reasons for their success.

It is not embarrassing to realize that you lack an important attribute that prevents you from achieving success and staying in the lead, but in contrast, it should encourage you to search for a field in which you could direct your creativity and knowledge. No one is good or can be the best at everything they do. The real challenge is finding something where you can maximize your creativity and potential, focus on that, and try to reach new heights with that. This will help renew and strengthen your nerve cells in a manner that helps you discover yourself and promote your self-confidence. In addition, this will help promote your potential and capabilities, and further empower you to discover more about yourself. Thus, you will be able to break any barriers that stand in your path. In fact, your movement is the secret behind your life and existence, through which you will be able to convey the secret of knowledge and its unknown aspects to the future generations.

Now, have institutions where the principle of teamwork is not applied, managed to achieve continuous and renewable super creativity? If yes, how did they do that? If no, why did they fail?

Most of the institutions based in the western part of the globe, whose cultures and civilizations are not deeply-rooted in team work, have managed to apply the principle nevertheless, because they possess the active elements of movement and have a desire to use them. Besides, they have the philosophy of not regretting their mistakes as long as they learn from them. For that reason, they were able to overcome this shortcoming and succeed in being creative in new fields. This, in turn, empowered them to achieve knowledge-based creativity, which promoted their competitiveness and superiority.

On the other hand, other environments have failed to achieve the same knowledge-based creativity because they needed integrated contribution not only from the parties concerned, but from all parties, institutions, and community organizations. They were unwilling to pick the philosophy of team work that was foreign to them. When there is a lack of teamwork, you will not be able achieve your goal, regardless of your sincerity or potential.

Is new knowledge of an individual or collective origin? What are the facts-based evidence?

As explained before, it could be said that knowledge is of an individual origin. We gave examples of the stories of Michael, the Brontë Sisters, the Second Carpenter and British TV host David Frost. Also, those extrapolating the movement of cognitive production and how it was generated across different times and civilizations will know that knowledge is of an individual origin. Knowledge has lit up the universe with individual creations. If it was not for knowledge, there wouldn't have been science, art, music, or discovery. Knowledge, creativity, and genius, contributed by Archimedes, Da Vinci, Shakespeare, Newton, Voltaire, Beethoven, Darwin, Charles Dickens, the Bronte sisters, Thomas Edison, Van Gogh, Einstein, Stephen Hawking, Steve Jobs, and Bill Gates. All these innovations (cognitive outputs) are individual innovations which did not move between individual tacit knowledge and collective tacit knowledge as presented in the knowledge spiral of Nonaka and Takuchi in their SECI model (knowledge creation model), which is the most well-known such model all over the world.

Accordingly, the fluctuation of knowledge between individual tacit and collective tacit knowledge was not the basic form through which the world knowledge brought its best production.

Thus, how are we to deal with the SECI model knowledge creation spiral in accordance with cognitive stem cells?

The SECI Model of Stem Cells Cognitive (SCC)

How is the knowledge spiral creation managed in accordance with SECI model and Stem Cells Cognitive theory? This is explained through the following table:

1 S	2 E
First Stage: Origination, formation or development **High/super speed cognitive stem cells in the stage of formation and maturity** It starts with high/super speed cognitive stem cells (individual) generated by the individual but not in a state of complete maturity. It is grasped by members of the group, for completing what the stages of formation lacks. Then it forms high/super speed cognitive stem cells (collective) to get to the socialization and formation stages with which it becomes qualified to externalize.	**The Second Stage: Stage Externalization** **(the newly born knowledge)** The newly born knowledge externalizes. Upon externalization, the requirements it needs to meet can be determined, so that it takes the complete form with which we can compete with others at a global level.
3 **C**	**4** **I**
The Third Stage: Completion or final composition and complexity of knowledge **(The newly born information takes a more complicated and integrated form)** The newly born information comes in this stage to the final stage of completion or modification, after which it will be ready for circulation and spreading across the organization lines as a whole.	**Fourth Stage: New cognitive stem cells are added to the cognitive container and becomes an additional part of its previous constituents.** This is the stage where the knowledge is put for global use and seeps into the cognitive configuration of the knowledge container for all workers in the organization and others from other organizations to the world for the benefit of everyone.

Table 2: Knowledge creation according to
the SECI model and SCC theory

The term knowledge here does not change between individual tacit knowledge and collective tacit knowledge. This is a misunderstanding. When the newly born knowledge comes out, it is still newly born, not explicit knowledge. We must not call it "knowledge" until it has reached its final stage. Generally, a newly born knowledge or new innovation is a subject of care and interest and it has to be upgraded to the stages wherein it is restructured to its final and integrate form, taking into account all considerations and orientations. This is why the third stage in **table 2** is called the stage of completion or final composition where this newly born knowledge is made applicable and known on a large scale, ready to compete with its peers at a global level, part of our intellectual capital and a value added to our market capital

It is logical that we maintain the spiral system of knowledge in a manner that guarantees that it can recycle itself so that this newly born knowledge becomes part of our cognitive component on the level of the organization or company as a whole. Then the newly established and proved knowledge can be accessible to all people and be part of their cognitive container as a new cognitive constituent (newly established cognitive stem cells), after which the cycle starts once again in the knowledge spiral system. This is the knowledge spiral model in accordance with the cognitive stem cells theory.

The ninth rule in knowledge construction

It is wrong to use the terms tacit knowledge and explicit knowledge within the parts of the cognitive structure.

We have proved this is a common mistake with negative effects on knowledge understanding and handling. Spiral knowledge does not oscillate between tacit knowledge and explicit knowledge or individual tacit knowledge and collective tacit knowledge. We have already corrected this mistake.

However, knowledge is between high/super speed cognitive stem cells originated individually, where the individual carries it until the maturity stage where it is still incomplete newly formed knowledge. Following that, the minds of the individuals within the group process it and add to it the complementary parts which did not existed in the formation and maturity stage, and then the group turn this output to an individually formed mature newly born knowledge, under the care of the group.

The reality of individuality and collectivity in the cognitive structure process

We have explained that knowledge birth and origination is an individual process. We cannot say that many individuals can produce this newly born knowledge. Those who propagandize this idea confound and confuse others as they do not understand the law of knowledge management. Knowledge is individually born and originated. No doubt that the group has a conclusively important role that we have already shed light on, with ample examples and evidence. Even if we work as a team, and even if we talk about the boundaries of the group, family, or the globally interested parties, since they are all present, it is critical to remember that they aren't there in time of knowledge origination.

We, as specialists, professionals or interested parties, are in a collective research, where each individual makes his/her mark and exert his/her respective efforts to solve a problem related to the collective work, in order to reach certain knowledge. If reached, it will help us all enter the market and overrun the competitors.

Let's go back to the details of the four stages in the foregoing SECI Model in accordance of the Cognitive Stem Cells Theory so that the structure in the method is easily understood.

First Stage: socialization, origination, formation or development of the newly born knowledge
The total energy of the team in this stage has an important role to play; it stimulates the individual, who is the knowledge bearer so they generate powerful newly born immature knowledge which will reach maturity under the care of the team members. Thus the cognition changes from socialization and individual formation to collective maturation.

The second Stage: externalization
In this stage, the newly born knowledge is externalized. It is explicit, so it undergoes examination and operation. It is accessible for other team members to complete its structure and transfer it to mature knowledge, however it is not independent enough to be offered and circulated in the global markets.

The third Stage: combination
In this stage, all the additional efforts are completed. With the new modifications, it turns to be more acceptable in terms of application and handling in comparison with the first form. This stage prepares the output for global competition and deployment and even prevalence over preceding peers. In this form, the newly born knowledge can

be pre-deployed, applicable, and accessible for all members in the organization that have produced it and the other global organizations.

The fourth Stage: internalization
The newly born knowledge becomes a new cognitive component for everyone in the organization and other relevant organizations, as well as on a global level. It is now added to previously formed knowledge, and internalized within everyone who uses it. This is where it is further modified or used as a basis for new knowledge in individuals. New knowledge turns anew to be new cognitive stem cells added to the already existed ones (in accordance with the cognitive walls). This stage represents an interpretation of the role of the new knowledge in mind building and brainstorming. New knowledge, as deduced from the above explanation, adds to the culture of the generations to come. It contributes in the discovery and development of talents and capabilities and the enrichment of mind and strengthening its nerve connectors, neurons, memory, and imagination.

Cognitive formation dimensions as per stem cells cognitive

The first dimension: It must be purely individual. This is essential in knowledge, creativity, and genius outputs, subject to the availability of cognitive environment. This requires an environment and a society with cognitive capabilities. We have provided many examples and explanations in this regard, for example the role of environment and community with Darwin.

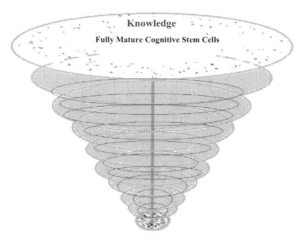

High/or Super Active Cognetive Steam Cells
Figure 32: The first dimension in the production
of knowledge by cognitive stem cells theory

Figure 32 represents the first dimension of the production of knowledge by cognitive stem cells theory. Formation began with cognitive stem cells of high / ultra-activity. These cells gathered and moved as a result of the cognitive movement and energy (electro-chemical-magnetic cognitive energy), which is emitted as a result of thinking, perception, imagination, connectivity, reasoning and recalling images, information and data, and all the cognitive components of the stem cell cognitive. All that reacts in a high constant perpetual motion or high activity; to bring to us the cognitive newborn.

The Second Dimension: It may be an individual within a team. This applies to specialty works and the works of organizations and companies, knowing that cognition is not collective as we had explained, however, the collective work is required only as complementary efforts to restructure the newly born knowledge.

The most suitable environment for this knowledge production is an environment whose people strongly believe in team work. Such an environment provides the best and most continuous cognitive outputs whose impact remains for subsequent generations.

Finance motivated energy, no matter how much, will never be equal to the energy motivated by the behavior, spirit, and desire of a team.

For example:

Compare between the cognitive creations outputted by Toyota and Apple. The comparison must be based on two important principles:

1. **The principle of total cognitive outputs** with non-stop production of 10 to 20 years.
2. **The cumulative cognitive effect** on the team members outputting the knowledge is no doubt of great importance as this has its clear positive impact on the generations to come, and this is what really matters in the balanced and integral cognitive structure.

Tenth rule in knowledge construction

The larger the total participation in the cognitive structure, the greater and clearer is the cumulative cognitive impact on the total of individuals and the present and future generations. Thus, the environments in which teamwork takes root in its culture are environments that are healthier and have much influential cognitive impact. Here, lies the secret of making authentic civilization.

First Principle: The total of the cognitive outputs of Toyota indicates that it is higher than Apple in terms of cognitive quantity and diversity in multiple areas such as administration, technology, deposits, sales, quality, monitoring, control, etc. This has had a positive impact on Toyota and its environments, as well as other generations and even the world, where some organizations circulated the Toyota approach, in terms of method, knowledge, innovation, theories, and systems, etc.

Second Principle: This will be clearer in the case of Toyota where the number of employees participating in cognitive outputs is incomparable to the number of employees performing the same at Apple. The number of employees producing knowledge at Toyota, includes the different categories, starting from simple employees to the highest level of administration. The number of creative groups from the base of the organization hierarchy may even surpass the number from the higher levels in the organizational hierarchy.

On the other hand, the cognitive outputs in Apple have been achieved by a few employees. The creative process at Apple from beginning to end is a unique process in terms of the high energy leadership and cognitive creativity represented in Steve Jobs. We cannot predict what will happen within the Apple organization within the following 10 – 20 years after the grave loss of Steve Jobs. However, according to our analysis Apple will not be the same without his management and creativity. Toyota, however, will never undergo dramatic changes in the field of its innovations, from the same fate, unless the global economy undergoes dramatic level of changes.

Simply, compare between the period in which Steve Jobs left Apple and the period in which he went back again, to know the effect of successful leadership on the cognitive outputs of Apple. As explained before, the Japanese environment as we pointed out, is one of the best environments in the collective knowledge production, despite the power of the creativity incentive or motive for the production of collective knowledge in other environments, whose culture is dominated by the individual character. In those, the collective cognitive production remains weak in the total of knowledge and its impact on future generations, compared with environments in which the spirit of community and collective production of knowledge are deeply rooted.

Third Principle: It is a good aspect of a company if it has a team of scientific researchers or specialized workers who work on extremely specialized scientific subjects, that need the whole team's collaboration to solve. An individual cannot represent the cognitive restructure alone. All team members have to participate in solving the subject matter in question. In the presence of an integrated team all puzzles can be decrypted. This is applicable in the scientific and medical research centers, and indicated in the outputs of research centers in the global universities, research centers, etc.

Fourth Principle: It is a good policy to prepare and train specialized individuals for collective knowledge production. This requires, before proceeding with cognitive structure processes, consolidating and empowering the team spirit, as well as extreme care to classify individuals according to their potentials, motivations, desires, and abilities. The wrong combination of potentials or characters working together could have a dangerous effect on the whole team. Such groups can be an obstacle that hinders and inhibits the capacities of others. Here, cognitive structure will be unfeasible and unreliable, whatever the size of the spending, stimulus, and technology used in this regard.

Notice that in the second and third principles the role of the community is to resolve the dilemmas that cannot be resolved by the individual alone due to the high potentials needed by the research topic or innovation which go beyond the individual's abilities. Examples are the physical, practical, and specialized capabilities, all of which cannot be achieved by an individual alone. As pointed out previously, the creations of Einstein, Newton, Darwin, and others, and the birth of new knowledge by them was within the scope of their encyclopedic potential and abilities, but also required the cohesion of the environment, community and scientific institutions so as to provide them with research, dedication, and creative environment.

How can we apply the first principle to produce knowledge in accordance with the cognitive stem cells theory? How does the individual move through his abilities, talents, and the energy of the surrounding environment, organizations, and public and community institutions?

This can be applied through a model exhibited by Newton. It is based on the individual based knowledge output, without collective intervention. This means that the cognitive structure process includes the following:

- Super-active cognitive stem cells (ultra-active): as in the case of intellectuals, discoverers, and researchers whose knowledge fueled the scientific and knowledge revolutions and changes in the human history. Their stem cells cognitive were ultra-active.
- Subsequently, this leads to the formation of the cognitive newborn (individually formed).

Let's explain this in more detail:
Newton's story started when his attention was attracted to an incident. He recalled his memories and cognitive components, i.e. the super-active cognitive stem cells including images, rules, equations, situations, and experiences which are part of his cognitive container. The recalling process happens, unintentionally, that is, without monitoring. The questions came as a consequence of an active mind, one after the other. The minds activity is not limited. It cannot be confined in place or time. Questions flow, looking for answers and difficult problems wait for solution. This may take a long time. Days, months, and even years could pass before reaching a solution to a difficult problem. However, at the end the day, the scientist reaches a solution, and a discovery, theory or a law is produced to solve the enigma. If he fails, another scientist proceeds with the research and reaches a solution, or if he fails, some third scientist proceeds with the same research. This is the law of knowledge and the secret behind it. It never surrenders easily. It doesn't give up its secret to others so easily. It never gives its secrets to all those who have qualifications, capabilities, cognitive components, information, data, experience, and practice. You may have all these, but with no avail. So, imagine what will happen if someone believes that

they have some of such talents and as a result have knowledge, or that they have the capability to make knowledge. **This is too difficult!**

This brings to the minds some questions.

- Are the enigma and big problems, whether medical, scientific or of any other type, that face researchers and scientists, only born at the time when scientists think about them, or have they been there since the universe was created, and they just got attracted to them? If so, why? What is the aim?
- Why does a certain discovery take place in a certain time, associated with perplexing questions and enigmas?
- There may be an unapparent relation between electricity and magnetism. This relation was discovered by the Danish scientist Maxwell after he had discovered the law of electromagnetism. Is there a relation between this discovery and the discoverer who could reach the enigma behind it?
- What enables the sperm to decode the cipher and reach the egg? How does the egg recognize the targeted sperm? How does the egg call the sperm? How does the egg select the sperm and throw the other sperms away?
- Does the secret of knowledge which attracts a certain type of people consist in the supposition that each thing in the universe has energy and has its equivalent frequency, thus there is a mutual attraction between the two as we explained through our analysis?

Let's get back to Newton, while we consider these questions. Three hundred and fifty years ago, that is, in 1665, a young man, Newton, was sitting under a tree, like hundreds and millions of people who sat under trees before or after him. Suddenly an apple falls from the top of the tree. Moved by his curiosity and astonishment, his mind starts thinking so deeply: why did the apple fell so? Why didn't the apple rise up, instead of going down? Brainstorming starts. This may be the password and the key to knowledge. Brainstorming brings to the surface all the cognitive stem cells. His curiosity would have never been satisfied until an answer had been found. Newton found that the power that attracted the apple to the ground is the same power that keeps the moon in its orbit; that is, gravitation. From a falling apple, Newton united the laws of the land and the laws of the heavens in a single theory; that is gravity. The laws of motion of the planets in their orbits are the same that control the tides and the fruit falling to the ground. This is the first force that is understood in a scientific manner. In fact, Newton opened the door to those who came after him. Civilizations have been built and scientific revolutions have started based on Newton's laws. Still his equations that describe the force give accurate scientific references, and represent an essential locus for scientists up to this day. Even in the field of forecasting the motion of rockets, scientists rely on the Newton's law and equations.

Knowledge will remain, like a queen, of high esteem. Never shall it submit its kingdom. It just reveals to us some of its charms and secrets in due measure, drop by drop and little by little, so that we remain thirsty for knowledge. In spite of all this Newton died without having the slightest idea about the mechanisms behind gravity, and how gravity work? Two hundred fifty years after Newton's death, the answer was finally decoded. This story illustrates how the dimensions were used to produce knowledge in accordance with the cognitive stem cells theory.

<u>Types of cognitive stem cells</u>

Not all cognitive stem cells have the energy that can help in forming the output of new knowledge, because of the high energy needed by new knowledge formation. The types of cognitive stem cells are:
1. The active cognitive stem cell
2. The high-active cognitive stem cells
3. The super-active cognitive stem cells
4. The neglected cognitive stem cells

1. The active cognitive stem cells

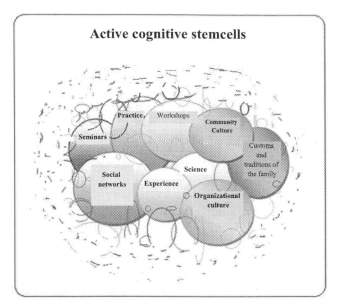

Figure 33: The active cognitive stem cells

As seen in **figure 33**, there is poor communication between the cognitive components in the active cognitive stem cells, as a result of the active chemical, electrical, magnetic, neurological, and cognitive movement. This does not allow for high-activity communication between cognitive components. This appears clearly through the scattered dots that represent the movement of communication between the cognitive components and the extent of their movement.

This type of cognitive stem cells is characterized by their ability to transform into high activity stem cells so that it can produce new knowledge, depending on the extent of attention of the connected neurological kinetic energy to thinking, imagination, and visualization. People who have this type of cognitive stem cells are interested only in questions related to their liking and trends in terms of science, hobby, art, literature, or their profession issues. The condition for producing knowledge for them is the qualification required for generating new knowledge. This is similar to what happened in the case of Michael, the second carpenter, and David Frost, the British programs presenter.

This type can be upgraded to the super-active type, on the condition that there is self-training and an expert that cares for the trainee and identifies the qualifications required for enabling the trainee to be upgraded on the basis of his cognitive capacity. Here also, it is required that the trend and desire, as we classified before, are super-active or upgradable by training, follow-up, and practice to such degree. In addition, there must be a suitable environment, social institutions, and society, as we indicated in the story of Darwin. These are important conditions to fulfill the required global cognitive output that is required for the making of civilizations.

2. The high-active cognitive stem cells

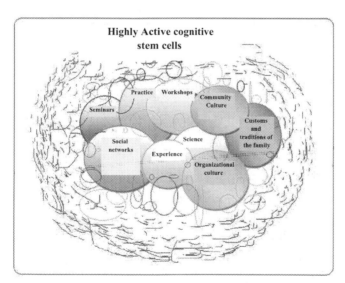

Figure 34: The high-active cognitive stem cells.
Red lines denote the communication between the
cognitive components and the environment.

Communication between the cognitive components is more dynamic and more active through the circular forms (red lines) around the cognitive components, which represent a higher neurological chemical movement. This reflects the ability of this type to produce knowledge without reaching the genius or super global production.

3. The super-active cognitive stem cells

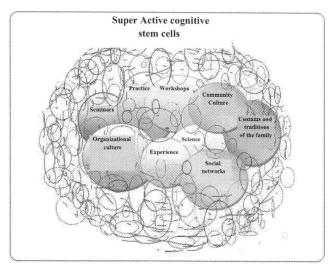

Figure 35: The super-active cognitive stem cells.
Red lines denote a higher level of communication,
between the cognitive components and the
environment, than high active cells.

Figure 35 indicates the electrical, chemical, magnetic, and neurological cognitive movement resulting from the continuous movement around a certain issue, subject, discovery or creation. This movement remains active until an extraordinary connection is reached, which excites each layer, component, inference, and connection between all components. This allows us to extract super quality components in terms of structure, energy, and frequency. This form produces a genius or innovation beyond all abilities, energies and talents. It is the global creativity and genius that goes beyond description and excellence.

4. The neglected cognitive stem cells

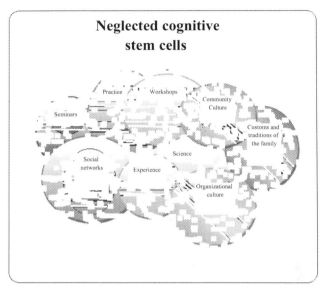

Figure 36: The neglected cognitive stem cells. Empty spaces denote a loss in communication between the cognitive components and the environment.

The movement and communication between the cognitive components seen above, have no longer been indicated (empty spaces). They have been replaced by depravity, intermittency, and in many cases decay and atrophy. Evidently this will continue unless we move and start refreshing knowledge. The tool required for this process is the super-active cognitive structure.

At the beginning of their formation, the active cognitive stem cells which are in the upgrading stage can be transformed into high-active cognitive stem cells, on condition that the individual has an active desire for upgrading and proceeds with good training. On the contrary, it is also possible that the cognitive stem cells at the formation stage undergo decline and deterioration when the cognitive nutrition that enables them to reach to maturity is suspended. The cells in this case turn to be neglected cells. This happens in either of the following scenarios:

The first includes emotional people, whose active movement is purely emotional, not based on talents. Their high chemical, electrical, magnetic, cognitive, neurological, and high-frequency energy is what drives them. This happens often around us. It occurs mainly in the adolescence phase which is characterized by unstable emotional motivation. It ensues due to the pressure of social surroundings, represented in parents and peers.

The second includes individuals who undergo severe psychological conditions which cause them depression and introversion. Such individuals either decline in terms of talents and knowledge, or challenge their difficult conditions and turn from weakness into extraordinary strength

However, this is beyond the scope of discussion on the transformation of active cognitive stem cells to neglected cognitive stem cells and will be dealt with in sequels to this book to look into the description and method of treatment of such cases.

Now, is it possible that super-active cognitive stem cells transform to neglected cognitive stem cells if the individual fails to control his talents and abilities in the same way he is accustomed to?

It is rare that this phenomenon occurs. It could happen in the case of a certain incident or disease that affects the memory totally or partially. This seldom happens, if we consider the extraordinary active movement between the neurological connectors in such individuals.

We should note here an important point: **Could it be that the cognitive movement and the cognition and knowledge birth is not enough to maintain the mind, in absence of cognitive diversity?**

The answer to this is a matter of importance. The human mind nowadays is not subjected to the same suffering that it was subjected to in the past. Today it is subjected to a multi-level assault on its talents, capacity, and energy. The assault of today dispels the human mind, disperses its defenses, weakens its ability to think deeply, and devastates all the tools that maintain its safety and vitality. These devastating forces are represented in **two factors:**

The first factor is modern technology which controls the mind's talents and mismanages the mind in a manner that disperses and devastates the mind. The modern technology misuses the minds of new generations in a manner that never guarantees maintaining their talents from being dispersed or forgotten. It is the main reason why the younger generations are turning away from reading or searching, that is, from thinking deeply, to the extent that nowadays most people would not be patient enough to read an SMS that is longer than one line. This has impacted the cumulative cognitive components held by the current generation. The future of the generations to come will be more dangerous as a result of this, because the knowledge that passes from the current generation to the coming generations is the output of the condition mentioned above. This is why it is necessary to rely on cognitive variety to maintain the mind and to enable it to produce creative and valuable cognitive outputs that can be the subject of competition at a global level.

The second factor is the lifestyle adopted today. Few people can be presently characterized by patience regarding reading, searching, creativity, and collecting valuable information that serve knowledge. This means that knowledge is limited to a few people whilst we actually need collective knowledge. The world suffers too much from this problem nowadays. It opens the doors for early Alzheimer's and other similar diseases. It is not strange then that younger and younger people suffer from such cognitive diseases. It is the responsibility of researchers, scientists, and leaders to reflect and work urgently on this problem. A rapid and effective action is urgently required because we are facing a problem of lack of cognitive structure, neurons' atrophy, and death of parts of the brain responsible for memory. These are the problems which are evident. There may be many more than we are not yet aware of. We fear that we may face a problem of human mind decay.

CHAPTER XI

In this Chapter:

- Knowledge as a container - it's true essence and it's secrets.
- The defect in cognitive structure and its reasons.
- The two major arms of knowledge.
- The eleventh rule in knowledge construction.
- The scientific evidence of the impact of the mind and its effects on the different body organs.

Knowledge as a container – what are its components?

What is the defect in cognitive structure and its reasons?
There are two major motives that have played an effective role in the emergence of this defect:

First: The pressure imposed by modern technology

Second: The incorrect handling of the concept of knowledge and constructing incorrect conclusions upon it.

1. The pressure imposed by modern technology

We have mentioned earlier that the pressure of modern technology has stifled the creativity and the free soul of knowledge. Constricting knowledge within the boundaries of information and statistics has resulted in that all the theories of knowledge have become solid based, thus making the whole cognitive structure dependent on these two factors.

We question whether scientific research lies under a similar stress or even more importantly: is it affected by the needs of whoever funds it? And what does this have to do with cognitive structure based research?

It's not a novel idea that scientific research lies under certain stressors. To illustrate this point let's look at the inspiring, international scientist Nina Jablonski.The American anthropologist expert, Professor Nina Jablonski, is the head of the Anthropology department at Pennsylvania University, and one of the most remarkable worldwide specialists in the field, who has spent over 20 years travelling around the world to find answers to her questions on skin color, like:

- When did it happen? Did it happen with the first existence of man on earth?

- Does temperature play a role in it?
- What's the secret behind the presence of darker skin colors around the equator?
- Is skin coloring a natural protection from the sun?
- Is protection from skin cancer the only reason behind this dark skin with all its variable tones?
- What is the direct relation between skin color and skin cancer that often occurs at old age? Does nature do that to protect us from skin cancer? Is that the whole story? Or is there a bigger secret?
- Is it not a mere protection from skin cancer? Could nature be doing that to preserve mankind?
- If so, what is the direct relation between skin color and preserving mankind?

This scientist, possessing a super active mind and highly intellectual stem cells, yearning for the birth of her intellectual baby and innovative discovery, has spent twenty years, never resting at one place, moving from barren lands to lonesome deserts, excavating, searching, investigating, examining, and scattering information. It's the active, vital and the energetic life of research. The life of those searching for the light, those who have denied their brain from staying dark and dull. If only we could sense the beauty of this life, the beauty of lighting up, even a small candle, to those who are coming from far away. It is a light for the following generations.

From question to question (here lies the essence and secret of knowledge): twenty years, in which she never rested for a single moment, until she took the lead in one of the most important discoveries of this age about skin color.

She questioned: why hasn't Darwin tackled this issue when discussing the essence of his theory around skin color and its reasons? Why haven't scientists in the previous centuries tackled this subject before? Why is there no precedent research concerning this matter, except for one interesting Italian scientist, Biazotee?

What Jablonski discovers is even more painful, and it is the point of our interest.[47]

In the early sixteenth centaury, Europeans started their expeditions to remote countries. Fair skinned Europeans encountered for the first-time people with darker skin colors when they visited those countries. Their entrance to these countries in Africa, Asia, the two Americas, and Australia were violent and brutal. They came with the creed that dark skin is a sign of degradation. They considered them savages with no morals. To them the darkening of the skin color is associated with inner darkness, the evil powers, and savageness. The native habitants everywhere were eliminated, or treated with unprecedented brutality in human history. To them, fair skin was a sign of elevation and transcending from darkness to light. Highly established ethics were always associated to the white man. Slavery, along with other benefits, was the reason behind promoting such ideologies until it became a firmly established European creed. By the eighteenth century, those beliefs were deeply rooted in the heart and soul of Europeans to the extent that it has affected the works of the earlier scientists, like the works of the Swedish scientist Carl Linnaeus who is the father of the science of taxonomy and the science of binomial nomenclature. In addition, he was the first to assort nations based on skin color. This creed remained with the Europeans in particular and westerns in general till the twentieth century, a remnant of it even extending to our modern time.

---

[47] Documentary: The skin color and racism_skinDeep_ARTESBS skinDee as amended by the author

The scientific community was conservative towards scholars who researched the evolution of skin color. It was considered a taboo which resulted in the delay of research related to this area and its important impact on us. Nina Jablonski's research found that skin color is not only for protection from ultraviolet rays and maintaining the synthesis of vitamin D, but also has vital importance in embryonic evolution.[48] Furthermore, its important relation to folic acid [49] which, if becomes deficient, leads to obvious brain atrophy. This is but a few of the results found by this amazing scientist who wandered around the world for twenty years hunting for answers to her questions.

This is the essence of knowledge; its secret, that provides you with energy, health, vitality, and competition. It's a hidden secret that you may only encounter if you start the continuous hunt that never ceases. The hunt for knowledge.

Before leaving the first motive, it's worth mentioning that modern technology has played a major effective role in accelerating the spread of intellectual knowledge around the world, which has had an incredible impact that can't be denied or derogated. Knowledge is now a revolving scientific investment. In fact, it is now playing a major role in the international economy, with various researches on the subject having a positive impact, especially in the business field for some of the leading major enterprises such as Hewlett-Packard, Toyota Apple, General Motors, General Electric, BP, and IBM.

Secondly, technology is playing a major role in the transitioning, the spreading, the enriching, and the archiving of the whole process of intellectual construction. We can't tackle the issue of intellectual construction on an integrated international level without referring to the technological construction.

---

[48] http://anth.la.psu.edu/people/ngj2
[49] https://en.wikipedia.org/wiki/Nina_Jablonski

2. The incorrect handling of the concept of knowledge and constructing incorrect conclusions upon it.

Knowledge has been handled from **the constituent perspective**, as previously clarified, via clear evidence and demonstration. Knowledge isn't crude components, whether we are dealing with a large or small number of components. Even if we managed to list and study them all individually we will not have valuable conclusions.

The majority of scientists, researchers and those interested in intellectual construction have handled it on the basis of components, believing that once those components were possessed, one is capable of establishing knowledge. A lot have failed, not due to deficiency in effort, research, precession, or intelligence, but rather due to rushing and lack of complete, balanced research as previously demonstrated, with all its causes and repercussions.

So, what is the real essence of the intellectual concept and its secrets which if we neglect or disregard, would not be able to attain the sought knowledge that we are working on constructing?

The two major arms of intellect

The first arm: The components which serves as the nutrient that will help in the growth of its cells and the formation of its layers until it finally grows and shapes the intellectual embryo.

The second arm: The tool, which is the mind (the cognitive container). It is the keynote player, the womb in which the sperm of knowledge attaches, and without which knowledge wouldn't have existed.

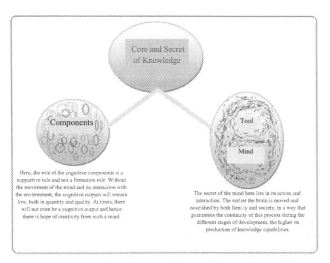

Here, the role of the cognitive components is a supportive role and not a formation role. Without the movement of the mind and its interaction with the environment, the cognitive outputs will remain low, both in quantity and quality. At times, there will not even be a cognitive output and hence there is hope of creativity from such a mind.

The secret of the mind here lies in its action and interaction. The earlier the brain is moved and nourished by both fami ly and society, in a way that guarantees the continuity of this process during the different stages of development, the higher its production of knowledge capabilities.

Figure 37: In this figure, the tool (mind) and the components of knowledge have been separated to express the role and nature of each arm, however, in reality there is no separate vessel for the components and the brain, they both exist in the same vessel: the vessel of knowledge.

As a reminder, when we use the term intellectual components, we are referring to the tools that help individuals understand what they recognize and pass through their senses, as well as the action of the brain. These can be for example people, pictures, shapes, situations or information. Hence whatever passes through our senses and has been grasped, analyzed, and can be summoned from our memory is in fact an intellectual component.

The means to handling both major arms of knowledge

Many are heading towards intellectual construction, in a simple, less stressful way as it doesn't overweigh them with the hustle of research or observation, assuming that this is the real cognitive structure. As a result, this makes them reduce their sense of responsibility and the pressure associated with trying to improve their cognitive structure by any means. This leads to unsatisfying and unexpected results which, especially in places of business, does not reflect the amount of money spent on trying to improve the intellectual construction of the firm.

The next question then becomes, even when successful knowledge construction is achieved, how will it be transmitted to employees?

To reiterate, the correct, integrated, and balanced cognitive structure is:

- A highly active and superior intellectual vessel (person).
- Knowledge components that are proportional to the high energy or motivation of the knowledge vessel (person).

Why is the approach towards gaining intellectual components wrong, and how does this play an effective role in the fundamental destruction of the intellectual construction?

To start with, it is important to explain to those who believe that collecting knowledge in all its forms and from all its sources is- on its own- the basis of cognitive structure. This is similar to believing that collecting all sorts of flowers and plants from a garden and putting them into a machine that would mix them and squeeze them to create honey would actually result in honey!

The continuous active movement of the honey bee is an example, where it visits 4 million flowers to make a pound of honey, while travelling actively for thousands of miles back and forth, telling the rest of the bee hive the location of the nectar, full of energy, and without any disdain for the work, co-workers or managers (queen bee). How many flowers and plants does it fertilize? One third of what we eat has been fertilized by honey bees. The secret of the honey bee doesn't merely lie in the honey. Some may say, it doesn't have managers like most people do, or it's not hunted by depression like we are, or it doesn't have to worry about annual appraisals which haunt us even in our sleep! The honey bee might not have problems similar to ours, but the problem it does have might be so much bigger – the Varroa. This predator sucks its blood, weakens it and can destroy its entire race. Hence, if it takes all this work to make honey, why would it be any easier when what we are trying to make is a sound mind? We are trying to construct the ability to meditate, consider, analyze, conclude, and resolve problems.

Knowledge is bigger and much more important. It is:

- A mind, or an intellectual vessel which is like the womb that creates knowledge
- Components and knowledge stem cells. Recall that a bee needs to fertilize 4 million flowers to produce only a pound of honey? Now, imagine how much knowledge we need to collect and shape into the knowledge component- the knowledge stem cell- to produce and create new knowledge that would lighten up our way. How do you prepare for that?

When there is activity inside the mind to gain knowledge, we have previously noted that this kind of activity is either:

- High-activity
- Super active

Since we are discussing the creation and production of knowledge on a competitive level, or on a level that would help us reach the international level, this is the only thing we can depend on.

Anything less, would result in the production of almost no new knowledge, beneath the level of international competition, and beneath the level of enhancing your capital of knowledge. It would definitely not be enough to raise your value in the market, as demonstrated by international companies who enhance their creativity as well as the creativity and knowledge of their employees, thus elevating their capital in the process.

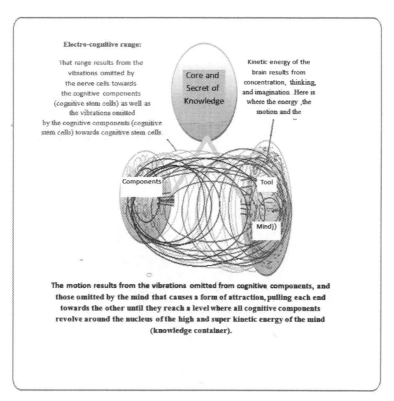

Figure 38: The movement arousing energy and vibrations
towards the knowledge component (knowledge stem cells)

The higher the intensity of the directed movement towards the
components of knowledge (stem cells of knowledge) the higher the
electro-chemical-neuro-electric charge of knowledge produced, forming
the attraction force for these components until they fully adhere with
the brain (tool).

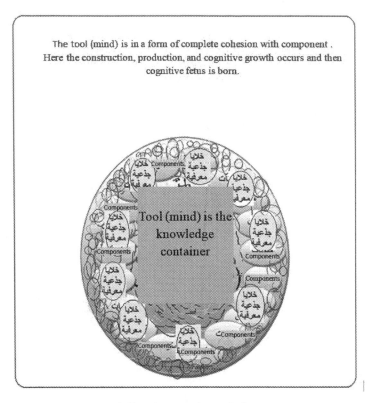

Figure 39: The ultimate knowledge container

If there is no kinetic energy inside the vessel of knowledge (the brain) then there will be no concentration, imagination, or thinking (mind working). That doesn't mean that the processor isn't really functioning, but rather it is not performing actively on a high occupational level or job position. It is only performing physical energy that would help it accomplish the assigned tasks. It isn't into knowledge or any of its forms. How will this person's brain approximately look like on basis of its components and imagination? The neurons would gradually atrophy and disintegrate with time, short term memory loss soon follows with all its consequences, varying in its level, speed and intensity.

The eleventh rule in knowledge construction

The greatest secret of knowledge is its vessel (the brain). It's the brain activity that gives it its real value and worth regardless of the size and variation of its components, otherwise we can save these components on a computer or any other tool of modern technology. The brain will always remain the key secret and the core of knowledge. We can't construct unless we establish a healthy key and secret of knowledge. Then and only then, comes the role of components.

Scientific evidence on the effect of the mind movement on its results and outputs

Here, is some of the scientific evidence on the effect of the mind movement, whether in thought or in search, excavation, imagination, perception, inference or connectivity.

A medical examination revealed that imagination can be used to change what we see or hear. Researchers at the Karolinska Institute, in Sweden explained that our imagination can affect how we deal with the exterior world in a way more than we could have ever perceived. The study sheds a new light on the traditional question of psychology and neurology and how we can combine stored information with different feelings. Professor Christopher Berger, neurologist at the Swedish institute, and supervisor on the research development section, asserted that we tend to deeply think about the things we imagine, which results in a change in our vision towards the things we see and hear around us. [50,51]

Active imagination

Imagining certain things may activate specific spots in the brain like the cortex, which is an important spot of feeling reception, that activates and stimulates almost real changes, relative to other parts of the brain, in order to stimulate physiological change.[52]

What happens when you imagine that you are tasting, touching or smelling something, or imagine that you are seeing someone you love? The mind and reaction get connected, thus awakening the nerve links to connect, which works on the maintenance, regeneration, and strengthening of the nerve cells. The more senses you use in a given imagination experiment, the stronger the physiological response is.[53] Conceptual imagination activates brain functions in a way similar to actual experiences. The eye movement is part of the visual conceptual imagination, and olfaction is accompanied by the olfactory brain image.[54]

Some of the physiological roles affected by conceptual imagination are:

- Heart rate speed.
- Artery blood pressure.
- The level of nerve links.
- Immunity.

---

[50] http://www.brainfacts.org/sensing-thinking-behaving/senses-and-perception/articles/2015/mysteries-of-the-brain-perceiving-brain/
[51] http://www.axonpotential.com/the-power-of-imagination/
[52] Achterberg, j.Imagery in Healing. Shambala Publications 1985
[53] Dossey,keegan,guzzetta.(2000) Holistic mursing a handbook for practice Maryland: Aspen publication.pp.539-579
[54] Bensafi, M.et al. (2003) Olfactomotor activity during imagery mimics that during perception. Nature Neuroscience, 6 (11): 1142-1144.

- Pain reduction.
- Anxiety.
- Mood

In case of perceptual awareness, some people can see the change in the reality of what they perceptually see, which we may call the mind's eye; while others who don't have visual thinking can't perceive this reality to change their world. Scientists have discovered, from a number of neurological experiments, that the spots continuously triggered becomes active, and increases in size and capacity compared to other spots. For example, research has proven that the hippocampus in the brain is larger in taxi drivers than it is in ordinary people, as they use it to promptly locate their clients' destination, all the while considering the alternative roads and identifying the fastest one of them. The continuous use of the hippocampus by taxi drivers for this recollection made it grow bigger than in others. Another example is the scientific experiments done on Einstein's brain that has discovered that his Xanthoma cells are 15% more than ordinary people. All in all, scientific research has proven that the effects of continuous brain movement on producing high level cognitive outputs.

Conclusion

As I sit here, preparing to put the final touches on this book, I did something extraordinary. I started to actively organize my home's office room, which no one knows about or enters, it's my studio, my workshop, my meditation room, and my office. I started to organize it the usual way, however, I went overboard and extended to reach the various corners of the room, I unconsciously found myself cleaning the floor! Cleaned the attached bathroom and replaced the sanitizer and the air freshener. My hands ran swiftly around the office cleaning and organizing everything in only 20 minutes. I noticed a weird thing; energy has exploded from within me as if I am listening to a happy cheerful melody playing inside of me. Here I remembered a story that I read before and that greatly touched me. It was the story of Professor Ernst Mayr, leading scientist in biology and honor professor at Harvard University. He was the winner of the highest Honor's degree in the field of evolutionary biology and the highest honor's degree in the history of science. He has reached the age of 90 and was still vibrant and energetic; looking at least a decade younger than his real age, giggling and talking about himself while being filled with energy. He was sharing the story of how a few days back when his helper was late and the kitchen floor needed cleaning, he got a bucket and cleaned it himself.

Why did Mayr feel so happy? Why did he not feel down or tired after he had consumed all this energy at this age, while others who may even be younger than him may feel exhausted and drained after using up maybe a little energy?

It suddenly struck me while cleaning right now. The secret that brought Mayr happiness, and many others who have taken the same path. It is the energy of intellect, its secret, and its frequency, when you willingly give it and search for it passionately. Its higher and more intense and extraordinary. The day you decide to exert it willingly the universe will answer to you stronger, melody after melody. The secret behind this happiness is the concurrence of both energies, and both frequencies. It's the secret of the universe, the secret of its motion, the secret of its fertility, the secret of its maturity, and the secret of its regeneration.

Exerting energy happily towards anything and making yourself feel this happiness will repay you with even more energy, more understanding, and more happiness, more than you could ever imagine.

Exert it, don't delay. It's out there waiting for you and calling for you to complete the melody of the universe. You will hear it, - approach, decide, and conquer.

Printed in the United States
By Bookmasters